MODERN WORLD LEADERS

Thabo Mbeki

MODERN WORLD LEADERS

Michelle Bachelet
Tony Blair
George W. Bush
Hugo Chávez
Jacques Chirac
Hu Jintao
Hamid Karzai
Ali Khamenei
Thabo Mbeki
Angela Merkel
Hosni Mubarak
Pervez Musharraf
Pope Benedict XVI
Pope John Paul II
Vladimir Putin
The Saudi Royal Family
Ariel Sharon
Viktor Yushchenko

MODERN WORLD LEADERS

Thabo Mbeki

Dennis Abrams

CHELSEA HOUSE
PUBLISHERS

An imprint of Infobase Publishing

Thabo Mbeki

Copyright © 2008 by Infobase Publishing

Chelsea House
An imprint of Infobase Publishing
132 West 31st Street
New York, NY 10001

Library of Congress Cataloging-in-Publication Data

Abrams, Dennis, 1960-
  Thabo Mbeki / Dennis Abrams
      p. cm. — (Modern world leaders)
  Includes bibliographical references and index.
  Audience: Grades 9-12.
  ISBN-13: 978-0-7910-9443-3 (hardcover)
  ISBN-10: 0-7910-9443-X (hardcover)
  1. Mbeki, Thabo—Juvenile literature. 2. Presidents—South Africa—Biography—Juvenile literature. 3. South Africa—Politics and government—1948—Juvenile literature. I. Title. II. Series.
  DT1975.A27 2007
  968.06'6092—dc22
  [B]   2007000899

Chelsea House books are available at special discounts when purchased in bulk quantities for businesses, associations, institutions, or sales promotions. Please call our Special Sales Department in New York at (212) 967-8800 or (800) 322-8755.

You can find Chelsea House on the World Wide Web at http://www.chelseahouse.com

Text design by Erik Lindstrom
Cover design by Takeshi Takahashi

Printed in the United States of America

Bang EJB 10 9 8 7 6 5 4 3 2 1

This book is printed on acid-free paper.

All links and Web addresses were checked and verified to be correct at the time of publication. Because of the dynamic nature of the Web, some addresses and links may have changed since publication and may no longer be valid.

TABLE OF CONTENTS

On Leadership

Leadership, it may be said, is really what makes the world go round. Love no doubt smoothes the passage; but love is a private transaction between consenting adults. Leadership is a public transaction with history. The idea of leadership affirms the capacity of individuals to move, inspire, and mobilize masses of people so that they act together in pursuit of an end. Sometimes leadership serves good purposes, sometimes bad; but whether the end is benign or evil, great leaders are those men and women who leave their personal stamp on history.

Now, the very concept of leadership implies the proposition that individuals can make a difference. This proposition has never been universally accepted. From classical times to the present day, eminent thinkers have regarded individuals as no more than the agents and pawns of larger forces, whether the gods and goddesses of the ancient world or, in the modern era, race, class, nation, the dialectic, the will of the people, the spirit of the times, history itself. Against such forces, the individual dwindles into insignificance.

So contends the thesis of historical determinism. Tolstoy's great novel *War and Peace* offers a famous statement of the case. Why, Tolstoy asked, did millions of men in the Napoleonic Wars, denying their human feelings and their common sense, move back and forth across Europe slaughtering their fellows? "The war," Tolstoy answered, "was bound to happen simply because it was bound to happen." All prior history determined it. As for leaders, they, Tolstoy said, "are but the labels that serve to give a name to an end and, like labels, they have the least possible connection with the event." The greater the leader, "the more conspicuous the inevitability and the predestination of every act he commits." The leader, said Tolstoy, is "the slave of history."

Determinism takes many forms. Marxism is the determinism of class. Nazism the determinism of race. But the idea of men and women as the slaves of history runs athwart the deepest human instincts. Rigid determinism abolishes the idea of human freedom—the assumption of free choice that underlies every move we make, every word we speak, every thought we think. It abolishes the idea of human responsibility, since it is manifestly unfair to reward or punish people for actions that are by definition beyond their control. No one can live consistently by any deterministic creed. The Marxist states prove this themselves by their extreme susceptibility to the cult of leadership.

More than that, history refutes the idea that individuals make no difference. In December 1931, a British politician crossing Fifth Avenue in New York City between 76th and 77th streets around 10:30 P.M. looked in the wrong direction and was knocked down by an automobile—a moment, he later recalled, of a man aghast, a world aglare: "I do not understand why I was not broken like an eggshell or squashed like a gooseberry." Fourteen months later an American politician, sitting in an open car in Miami, Florida, was fired on by an assassin; the man beside him was hit. Those who believe that individuals make no difference to history might well ponder whether the next two decades would have been the same had Mario Constasino's car killed Winston Churchill in 1931 and Giuseppe Zangara's bullet killed Franklin Roosevelt in 1933. Suppose, in addition, that Lenin had died of typhus in Siberia in 1895 and that Hitler had been killed on the western front in 1916. What would the twentieth century have looked like now?

For better or for worse, individuals do make a difference. "The notion that a people can run itself and its affairs anonymously," wrote the philosopher William James, "is now well known to be the silliest of absurdities. Mankind does nothing save through initiatives on the part of inventors, great or small, and imitation by the rest of us—these are the sole factors in human progress. Individuals of genius show the way, and set the patterns, which common people then adopt and follow."

Leadership, James suggests, means leadership in thought as well as in action. In the long run, leaders in thought may well make the greater difference to the world. "The ideas of economists and political philosophers, both when they are right and when they are wrong," wrote John Maynard Keynes, "are more powerful than is commonly understood. Indeed the world is ruled by little else. Practical men, who believe themselves to be quite exempt from any intellectual influences, are usually the slaves of some defunct economist. . . . The power of vested interests is vastly exaggerated compared with the gradual encroachment of ideas."

But, as Woodrow Wilson once said, "Those only are leaders of men, in the general eye, who lead in action. . . . It is at their hands that new thought gets its translation into the crude language of deeds." Leaders in thought often invent in solitude and obscurity, leaving to later generations the tasks of imitation. Leaders in action—the leaders portrayed in this series—have to be effective in their own time.

And they cannot be effective by themselves. They must act in response to the rhythms of their age. Their genius must be adapted, in a phrase from William James, "to the receptivities of the moment." Leaders are useless without followers. "There goes the mob," said the French politician, hearing a clamor in the streets. "I am their leader. I must follow them." Great leaders turn the inchoate emotions of the mob to purposes of their own. They seize on the opportunities of their time, the hopes, fears, frustrations, crises, potentialities. They succeed when events have prepared the way for them, when the community is awaiting to be aroused, when they can provide the clarifying and organizing ideas. Leadership completes the circuit between the individual and the mass and thereby alters history.

It may alter history for better or for worse. Leaders have been responsible for the most extravagant follies and most monstrous crimes that have beset suffering humanity. They have also been vital in such gains as humanity has made in individual freedom, religious and racial tolerance, social justice, and respect for human rights.

There is no sure way to tell in advance who is going to lead for good and who for evil. But a glance at the gallery of men and women in MODERN WORLD LEADERS suggests some useful tests.

One test is this: Do leaders lead by force or by persuasion? By command or by consent? Through most of history leadership was exercised by the divine right of authority. The duty of followers was to defer and to obey. "Theirs not to reason why/Theirs but to do and die." On occasion, as with the so-called enlightened despots of the eighteenth century in Europe, absolutist leadership was animated by humane purposes. More often, absolutism nourished the passion for domination, land, gold, and conquest and resulted in tyranny.

The great revolution of modern times has been the revolution of equality. "Perhaps no form of government," wrote the British historian James Bryce in his study of the United States, *The American Commonwealth*, "needs great leaders so much as democracy." The idea that all people should be equal in their legal condition has undermined the old structure of authority, hierarchy, and deference. The revolution of equality has had two contrary effects on the nature of leadership. For equality, as Alexis de Tocqueville pointed out in his great study *Democracy in America*, might mean equality in servitude as well as equality in freedom.

"I know of only two methods of establishing equality in the political world," Tocqueville wrote. "Rights must be given to every citizen, or none at all to anyone . . . save one, who is the master of all." There was no middle ground "between the sovereignty of all and the absolute power of one man." In his astonishing prediction of twentieth-century totalitarian dictatorship, Tocqueville explained how the revolution of equality could lead to the *Führerprinzip* and more terrible absolutism than the world had ever known.

But when rights are given to every citizen and the sovereignty of all is established, the problem of leadership takes a new form, becomes more exacting than ever before. It is easy to issue commands and enforce them by the rope and the stake, the concentration camp and the *gulag*. It is much harder to use argument and achievement to overcome opposition and win consent. The Founding Fathers of the United States understood the difficulty. They believed that history had given them the opportunity to decide, as Alexander Hamilton wrote in the first Federalist Paper, whether men are indeed capable of basing government on "reflection and choice, or whether they are forever destined to depend . . . on accident and force."

Government by reflection and choice called for a new style of leadership and a new quality of followership. It required leaders to be responsive to popular concerns, and it required followers to be active and informed participants in the process. Democracy does not eliminate emotion from politics; sometimes it fosters demagoguery; but it is confident that, as the greatest of democratic leaders put it, you cannot fool all of the people all of the time. It measures leadership by results and retires those who overreach or falter or fail.

It is true that in the long run despots are measured by results too. But they can postpone the day of judgment, sometimes indefinitely, and in the meantime they can do infinite harm. It is also true that democracy is no guarantee of virtue and intelligence in government, for the voice of the people is not necessarily the voice of God. But democracy, by assuring the right of opposition, offers built-in resistance to the evils inherent in absolutism. As the theologian Reinhold Niebuhr summed it up, "Man's capacity for justice makes democracy possible, but man's inclination to justice makes democracy necessary."

A second test for leadership is the end for which power is sought. When leaders have as their goal the supremacy of a master race or the promotion of totalitarian revolution or the acquisition and exploitation of colonies or the protection of greed and privilege or the preservation of personal power, it is likely that their leadership will do little to advance the cause of humanity. When their goal is the abolition of slavery, the liberation of women, the enlargement of opportunity for the poor and powerless, the extension of equal rights to racial minorities, the defense of the freedoms of expression and opposition, it is likely that their leadership will increase the sum of human liberty and welfare.

Leaders have done great harm to the world. They have also conferred great benefits. You will find both sorts in this series. Even "good" leaders must be regarded with a certain wariness. Leaders are not demigods; they put on their trousers one leg after another just like ordinary mortals. No leader is infallible, and every leader needs to be reminded of this at regular intervals. Irreverence irritates leaders but is their salvation. Unquestioning submission corrupts leaders and demeans followers. Making a cult of a leader is always a mistake. Fortunately hero worship generates its own antidote. "Every hero," said Emerson, "becomes a bore at last."

The single benefit the great leaders confer is to embolden the rest of us to live according to our own best selves, to be active, insistent, and resolute in affirming our own sense of things. For great leaders attest to the reality of human freedom against the supposed inevitabilities of history. And they attest to the wisdom and power that may lie within the most unlikely of us, which is why Abraham Lincoln remains the supreme example of great leadership. A great leader, said Emerson, exhibits new possibilities to all humanity. "We feed on genius. . . . Great men exist that there may be greater men."

Great leaders, in short, justify themselves by emancipating and empowering their followers. So humanity struggles to master its destiny, remembering with Alexis de Tocqueville: "It is true that around every man a fatal circle is traced beyond which he cannot pass; but within the wide verge of that circle he is powerful and free; as it is with man, so with communities." ●

1

Introduction

FOR THABO MBEKI, AS FOR MOST SOUTH AFRICANS, JUNE 16, 1999, WAS A day of mourning. It was also a day of celebration.

In South Africa, June 16 is Soweto Day. This is the date that is put aside to remember those killed during the Soweto Uprising. In 1976, thousands of black students met for a peaceful rally to protest the Afrikaans Medium Decree of 1974, which forced all black students to learn the Afrikaans language. Most students of color resented this decree, feeling that the Afrikaans language was the language of the white minority that had restricted their rights and forced them to live lives that were separate but unequal.

The unarmed student protestors were met by policemen fully equipped with weapons and tear gas. When the police threw canisters of tear gas to break up the students, a few of the students began throwing rocks back in retaliation. The

Hundreds of people were killed and more than a thousand were injured in the Soweto Uprising in June 1976. Police attacked student demonstrators who were peacefully protesting apartheid, and continued to hunt them in the streets of the city after the demonstrations escalated into rioting. To honor the dead and celebrate the freedom achieved, Soweto Day is commemorated every June 16 in South Africa.

majority of the students continued protesting peacefully, singing and waving signs.

When a white male police officer drew his gun and fired, panic erupted among the students. They began running, and the police began shooting. Riots broke out, and by the end of the day, 23 people, including 3 whites, had died.

The next day, 1,500 heavily armed police offers were sent into Soweto with high-powered weapons, including automatic rifles, stun guns, and carbines. They patrolled the streets in armored vehicles with helicopters flying overhead doing surveillance. White South African policemen fired their weapons indiscriminately in their efforts to retake control of the streets.

By the time the riots ended on June 18, between 200 and 600 people were dead. Thousands more were wounded. Many people view the Soweto Uprising as the beginning of the end of white apartheid rule. The murder of unarmed students encouraged many other black citizens to resist. Many white citizens as well turned away from their government, appalled at its actions.

So while June 16 was a day of mourning the dead, it was also a reason for celebrating the freedom they helped bring about. And that is why June 16 is now Inauguration Day in South Africa, and the day that Thabo Mbeki was sworn in as South Africa's second democratically elected president.

June 16, 1999, was also a day of historic transition in South African politics. Nelson Mandela, a hero to millions worldwide for his commitment to nonviolence and the man who had become the human face of resistance against apartheid, South Africa's first democratically elected president, was leaving office. Nearly 81 years old, he had earned the right to retire with honor. He had devoted his entire life to restoring the rights of black citizens of his country, spending 27 years in prison for his commitment to freedom.

An activist and leader of the African National Congress (ANC), Mandela had devoted his life to ending apartheid in South Africa and had been tried and imprisoned for his involvement in underground armed resistance activities. For Mandela and the ANC, armed struggle was a last resort; throughout his life he has remained committed to nonviolence.

Thabo Mbeki listens to the South Africa national anthem during commemorations for the thirtieth anniversary of the Soweto Uprising in June 2006. Though exiled from his beloved home country for nearly three decades, Mbeki has devoted his life to ending apartheid and creating a democratic South Africa.

During his imprisonment, Mandela had become the world's most widely known figure for his opposition to apartheid. Upon his release from prison in 1990, his determination to bring about reconciliation between both races, rather than resort to violence and revenge, helped to bring about a peaceful transition from apartheid to representative democracy in South Africa.

In fact, Thabo's own father, Govan Mbeki, had devoted his life to the cause of South African freedom as well, and served

FOR A TOTAL OF 28 YEARS, THABO MBEKI WAS UNABLE TO RETURN HOME TO HIS FAMILY, FRIENDS, AND BELOVED COUNTRY.

23 years in prison along with Nelson Mandela. It was from his father that Thabo learned the political lessons that committed him to the cause of freedom and ultimately brought him to the office of the presidency. As he once said, quoted on the Web site of the African National Congress, "I was born into the struggle."

Indeed, he sacrificed much to help bring an end to apartheid and freedom for his people. While growing up, he was forced to live away from home, and was largely raised by friends and family for fear that his parents would be arrested for their activities. Years later, he was forced to flee South Africa to live in exile; first to study, and then to help organize the resistance. For a total of 28 years, Thabo Mbeki was unable to return home to his family, friends, and beloved country.

Family members were lost to him as well. Not only did his father spend almost one-quarter of his life in prison, but Thabo's brother, Jama Mbeki, his son, Kwanda Mbeki, and his cousin, Phindile Mfeti, all disappeared during the apartheid era. To this day, the family does not know what happened to them.

As president, Thabo Mbeki hoped to help his nation recover from the ugliness of its past, and make a smooth transition into the twenty-first century. His time in office, however, has not been without its controversies, as many of his policies have come under attack.

Who is Thabo Mbeki? How did this son of a politician, born in a small South African village, go on to help bring about the end of apartheid and, ultimately, be chosen as the nation's president?

2

A Brief History of South Africa

IT IS IMPOSSIBLE TO UNDERSTAND A COUNTRY'S PRESENT WITHOUT UNDER-standing its past. It would be just like opening a book in the middle and starting to read from there—how could you really know what was going on? For example, it is difficult to understand the relationship between blacks and whites in the United States today without knowing about the country's history of slavery, segregation, and Jim Crow laws, and the progression into the Civil Rights Movement of the 1950s and 1960s.

It's the same thing with regard to South Africa. Like any other person, Thabo Mbeki is a product of his country's history and culture. One cannot fully understand the life and times of Thabo Mbeki without having some knowledge of his country's past. We must begin by seeing how South Africa's history created the world in which Mbeki grew up.

EUROPEAN EXPEDITIONS

In 1488, the Portuguese explorer Bartolomeu Dias sailed southward in the Atlantic Ocean, looking for a route to India. When he finally sailed around the southern tip of Africa into the Southern Indian Ocean, he became the first European to do so since ancient times. Other Portuguese explorers followed in his wake, including Vasco da Gama, who became the first person to sail directly from Europe to India during 1497–1499.

New name notwithstanding, it was not until 1652 that the Dutch set up the first permanent station at the Cape of Good Hope. (This station wasn't a full colony, just a station to supply passing ships with fresh water and vegetables.) This "supply depot" developed into the Cape Colony over the next 200 years.

None of these Portuguese explorers settled the area. Southern Africa was considered too dangerous for European sailors, let alone settlers. The Cape itself was originally known as the "Cape of Storms" because it was so dangerous for sailing ships. It was the British explorer Sir Francis Drake who, while circling the Cape in 1580, returning home from his voyage around the world in his ship, the *Golden Hind,* renamed it the "Cape of Good Hope." He reputedly said that, "No longer shall this be called the Cape of Storms, for it is the fairest Cape of them all."

New name notwithstanding, it was not until 1652 that the Dutch set up the first permanent station at the Cape of Good Hope. (This station wasn't a full colony, just a station to supply passing ships with fresh water and vegetables.) This "supply depot" developed into the Cape Colony over the next 200 years.

It is important to note that this land was not empty of people when the Europeans arrived. The area was already fully populated with Africans who had been there for tens of thousands of years. The bushmen were probably the first modern people to migrate to the southern tip of the African continent. It is estimated that when the Europeans arrived, the bushmen had been there for at least 25,000 years, perhaps even as long as 40,000 years. Eventually settling along the coast, they became known as the Khoikhoi.

At about the same time the Khoikhoi were setting up farms on the coast, the Bantu-speaking people also began arriving in

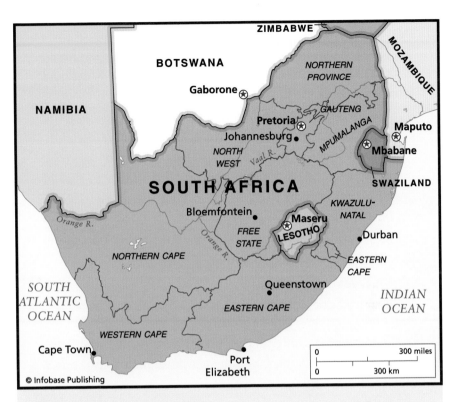

Map of South Africa and its states.

South Africa. The Bantu-speakers not only had domestic ani-mals and practiced agriculture, but they had skill in working iron and lived in settled villages. Some of these Bantu groups preferred to live near the coast. Others eventually settled in the Highveld (the higher-level grasslands). All of the native-born groups, bushmen, Khoikhoi, and Bantu-speakers, lived together peacefully.

The people of the new Dutch settlement, based at what would become the modern city of Cape Town, out of necessity traded with the neighboring Khoikhoi. Relations between the groups could not be called friendly, and the Dutch did what they could do to keep contact to a minimum.

One way they did this was to begin building their own farms. By growing their own crops, they would be able to minimize their dependency on the Khoikhoi. The small group of "free burghers," as these farmers were called, steadily grew. They began to expand their farms farther north and east into the Khoikhoi's territory, driving the Khoikhoi from their lands.

The majority of these burghers were of Dutch ancestry and belonged to the Calvinist Reformed Church of the Netherlands. As they continued to move north and east away from the coast, many began to take up a seminomadic life, similar to that of the Khoikhoi they had displaced. In addition to their herds, a family might own just a wagon, a tent, a Bible, and always a few guns. These were the first of the Trekboers (Wandering Farmers, later shortened to Boers).

They lived independently of any government. They were self-sufficient and isolated from other influences. This rough-and-ready lifestyle created a group of courageous individualists not too different from that of the American pioneers. They knew the land well, and based their lives on their main source of guidance, the Bible.

With the expansion of farms came a need for additional laborers. Large numbers of slaves began to be imported into South Africa, mainly from the Dutch-controlled areas of Madasgascar and Indonesia. These slaves often married Dutch settlers, and their descendants became known as "Cape Coloureds" and the "Cape Malays."

The growth of the Dutch population caused further expansion into Khoikhoi lands. Many Khoikhoi died from European diseases from which they had no natural immunity. Others were killed when they tried to fight back in a brave attempt to control their own lands. Most of the few remaining survivors were left with no other option but to work for the Europeans in an arrangement that was little better than slavery. Over time, the Khoikhoi, their European overseers, and the imported slaves became racially mixed. The offspring of these unions formed the basis for what became known as the Coloured population.

THE BRITISH

Dutch military and economic power began to fade by the end of the eighteenth century, and the British quickly moved in to fill the void. They seized the Cape in 1795 to keep it from falling into the hands of their rivals, the French. In 1803, the British briefly lost the Cape back to the Dutch before winning final recognition of their rule of the area in 1814.

At the tip of the continent, the British established a colony of 25,000 slaves, 20,000 white colonists, 15,000 Khoisan, and 1,000 freed black slaves. All economic and political power was held by the white elite. Strict legal and social boundaries were maintained between the races.

Like the Dutch, the British initially had little interest in the Cape Colony, other than as an important port. But things changed when a border dispute broke out between the Boers and the Xhosa on the colony's eastern frontier. At that time, the British convinced 5,000 immigrants to leave England and settle on land between the feuding groups, in an attempt to provide a buffer zone.

The plan didn't work. Most of the British settlers quickly fled the countryside for towns and cities. But one unintended consequence of the influx of British settlers was to disrupt the relative unity of white South Africa. Previously, the Boers and their ideas had gone largely unchallenged. Now there were two white language groups and cultures. A gap grew between the two groups as the English-speakers became the people of the cities, dominating politics, trade, finance, mining, and manufacturing. The Dutch and Afrikaans-speaking Boers remained relatively uneducated, living on farms in the countryside.

This gap between the British and the Boers grew even wider in 1833, when the British abolished slavery throughout their empire and therefore within the colony. This move angered the Boers, who, because of their rigid interpretation of the Bible, felt that they had a God-given superiority and power over other so-called "lesser" races.

Unhappy with British rule of the Cape Colony, and angry at the British proclamation of the equality of the races, several groups of Boers, along with their servants, left for the interior of the country in search of greater independence. This movement became known as the Great Trek. North and east of the Orange River (which formed the Cape Colony's frontier) these Voortrekkers ("Pioneers") found vast tracts of largely uninhabited grazing lands. They believed that this was their version of the Promised Land.

They originally settled into the area known as Natal, but left after the British annexed the area in 1843, a move that further angered the Boers. As the Boers continued moving north, the British settled into the Natal area. Needing labor, the British turned to their colony of India for manpower. Over the next 50 years, more than 150,000 indentured Indians arrived as well as numerous free "passenger Indians." They eventually became the largest Indian community outside of India. In fact, Mahatma Gandhi first made a name for himself in South Africa working for civil rights for Indians living there, before returning home to India to lead the movement for Indian independence.

Meanwhile, the Boers continued in their search for land and freedom, finally establishing themselves in the Transvaal and in the Orange Free State. At first it appeared that they would become stable, independent states, but the discovery of diamonds near Kimberley changed everything.

The first diamonds came from lands belonging to the Griqua (one of the best known of the Khoikhoi groups) but that were claimed by both the Transvaal and Orange Free State. Once again flexing their considerable muscle, the British stepped in and resolved the issue by claiming the territory for themselves.

The discovery of the diamond mines brought a fresh flood of European and black laborers into the area. Mining towns sprang up; the inhabitants ignored what the Boers felt was the

This engraving dating from 1837 shows the Great Trek made by Boers from the Cape Colony to Natal. In their quest for land and freedom from British rule, these Voortrekkers ended up in a full-fledged war.

"proper" separation of both white and black citizens. Adding to their frustrations, the Boers were furious that they had missed out on the economic benefits of the mines. The long-growing Boer anger was about to explode.

THE FIRST ANGLO-BOER WAR

The Boers' long-standing resentment of the British turned into full-blown rebellion in the Transvaal (which had been under British control since 1877), and the first Anglo-Boer War, known to Afrikaners as the "War of Independence," broke out in 1880. The conflict ended quickly with a huge Boer victory at the Battle of Majuba Hill on February 27, 1881. The republic

Men work 2,000 feet underground at the Kimberley Diamond Mine in South Africa at the turn of the twentieth century. The discovery of diamonds in the area resulted in more anguish for the resentful Boers, and was another factor fueling their rebellion.

gained its independence as the *Zuid-Afrikaansche Republiek* ("South African Republic"), or ZAR.

The British saw their defeat in the first Anglo-Boer War as merely a temporary setback. Their goal remained a federation of all the South African colonies and republics. They saw this as the best way to deal with the reality of a white Afrikaner majority. They also felt it would be the best way to promote their larger strategic interests in the area.

GOLD AND THE SECOND ANGLO-BOER WAR

In 1866, an Australian prospector discovered gold in the Witwatersrand Mountains, near Johannesburg in ZAR. The city's population grew to almost 100,000 by the mid-1890s, with the Boers once again being pushed to the sidelines. The British tried to gain control of the mines and failed, but it was apparent to the Boers that their republic was once again in danger.

The situation came to a head in 1899 when the British demanded that the 60,000 foreign whites working on the Witwatersrand be given voting rights. President Paul Kruger of the ZAR refused, calling for the withdrawal of British troops from the ZAR's borders. When the British refused, Kruger declared war.

This second Anglo-Boer War lasted longer than the first, and the British were much better prepared. By June of 1900, the last of the major Boer towns, Pretoria, had surrendered to the British. Resistance by the Boers continued for two more years with guerilla-style battles, and the British fought back equally hard.

By 1902, nearly 26,000 Boers had died of disease and neglect in British concentration camps. On May 31, 1902, the Treaty of Vereeniging was signed; the Boer republics acknowledged British sovereignty; and the British committed to rebuild the areas under their control that had been ravaged by war.

After two tough wars, the British turned their attention to rebuilding the country. By 1907, the mines of the Witwatersrand produced almost one-third of the world's gold production. But the peace between the two parties, the British and the Boers, was constantly being threatened.

The Afrikaners found themselves as poor farmers in a country dominated by big mining companies and foreign money. The British made many attempts to make them into Englishmen, including several failed attempts to make English

British troops prepare artillery to fire against the Boers, during the first Anglo-Boer War. The Boer victory achieved their independence from the British, but it was short lived. A second, longer war returned rule to Britain.

the official language of schools and the workplace. But because of this, the Boers held even more tightly to themselves and came to see Afrikaans as the "people's language" and a symbol of Afrikaner nationhood.

The British decided that it was time for South Africa to unite as one nation. The South Africa Act of 1909 brought the British-dominated areas of Cape Colony and Natal together with the formerly independent Boer republics of the ZAR and the Orange Free State. The Union would remain British territory, but with home rule for the Afrikaners.

English and Dutch became the official languages. (Afrikaans did not become an official language until 1925.) Black and coloured residents were not allowed to vote or to serve in parliament. The Union of South Africa was now in place, and the age of apartheid was about to begin.

3

The Age of Apartheid

ALTHOUGH BLACK CITIZENS MADE UP OVER 75 PERCENT OF THE POPULATION, they had no place in the newly formed Union of South Africa, where their human and political rights were gradually stripped away. Black people were not allowed to vote, since the white minority knew that, if given the vote, the black majority could run the government. A series of increasingly oppressive laws was also passed, making the already difficult lives of the black citizens even more difficult.

Black workers were not allowed to go on strike, serve in the military, or hold skilled jobs, which were reserved for whites. Restrictive pass laws were enacted, making it illegal for black people to move freely from one place to another.

In 1913, parliament enacted the Natives Land Act, which set aside a mere 8 percent of the country's land to be occupied by black citizens. This allowed white people, who made up only 20 percent of the population, to hold 90 percent of the land. Under this same law, black Africans could not rent land or even work as sharecroppers outside of their designated areas. The authorities evicted thousands of so-called squatters from farms and forced them into increasingly overcrowded and impoverished reserves, or into the cities.

Black and coloured opposition began to organize. The era saw the origination of the South African Native National Congress, known from 1923 on as the African National Congress (ANC). The ANC rapidly became the predominant black organization fighting the apartheid regime.

As time passed, Afrikaner nationalism continued to grow. Afrikaans replaced Dutch as an official language of the Union and the so-called *swart gevaar* (black threat) became the dominant issue of the 1929 election and of most future elections. The Afrikaners, the predominant white group, felt that they had a God-given right to rule South Africa. They played on this, as well as on a deep-rooted Afrikaner fear of living under black majority rule, to win elections.

From 1948 to 1994, the South African government was dominated by the Afrikaans National Party. The main policy of this government was apartheid, which means, literally, "apartness" in Afrikaans and Dutch. Under apartheid, people were legally classified into racial groups—the main ones being White, Black, Indian, and Coloured. The groups were then geographically, and forcibly, separated from each other on the basis of this legal classification. Black South Africans, in particular, became legal citizens of particular "homelands" that were supposedly independent nations within South Africa. Actually, though, they functioned more like U.S. Indian reservations, still under the control of the South African government.

But in reality, the vast majority of black South Africans never resided in these "homelands." In order to have any chance of earning a living, they would have to go work for white people in the "white" areas of South Africa. This prevented them from having any vote or influence, because the only place they had any rights at all was in their fictional homelands.

Laws were devised to cover every aspect of life, and to separate the races in every way imaginable. The following list describes some of the major laws enacted.

1. It was against the law for a white person to have any sexual relations with a person of a different race.

2. The Population Registration Act (1950). Citizens had to be registered as Black, White, or Coloured. If there was any question about what category one fit in, a classification board existed to rule on difficult cases. Minor officials would administer tests to determine if someone should be labeled either Coloured or Black, or if another person should be categorized as Coloured or White. Different members of the same family could find themselves in different racial groups. Further tests were given to determine membership of the various sub-racial groups of the Coloureds.

3. The Group Areas Act (1950) partitioned the country into different areas, with different areas being devoted to different racial groups. This law was the very heart of apartheid, because it was the basis upon which political and social separation was to be constructed.

4. The Reservation of Separate Amenities Act (1953) prohibited people of different races from using the same public facilities, such as drinking fountains, restrooms, etc.

5. The Promotion of Black Self-Government Act (1958) set up separate territorial governments in the "homelands." It designated lands for black people where they could have a vote. The aim was that these "homelands" or "Bantustans" would eventually become independent

This photograph shows a segregated store in South Africa in 1925. Much like the Black Codes that ordered separate facilities for blacks and whites in the American South, South Africa operated under a policy of a legal separation of the races. Unlike U.S. segregation, however, apartheid was in effect until the end of the twentieth century.

of South Africa. In practice, however, the South African government controlled these so-called separate states, even after some of them became "independent."

6. The Black Homeland Citizenship Act (1970) changed the status of the inhabitants of the "homelands" so that they were no longer citizens of South Africa. This was done to

guarantee that white [citizens] would become the demographic majority within "white" South Africa.

The upshot of these laws was that the black majority lived completely under the thumb of the white minority. Black and coloured South Africans were forced to carry identity documents. These documents were a sort of "passport" that stopped migration of black people into "white" South Africa. Black citizens were prohibited from living in (or even visiting) "white" towns without specific permission.

For black people, living in the cities was normally restricted to those who were employed in the cities by white people. Direct family relatives were not included, so wives often were separated from their husbands. Parents often were separated from their children.

Living under apartheid was a never-ending nightmare for black South Africans. They were not allowed to run businesses or professional practices in areas designed as "white South Africa." Anyone caught without a valid pass was subject to arrest and trial, and was then often deported to the person's nominal homeland.

Black areas rarely had plumbing or electricity. Hospitals and ambulances were segregated. The Bantu Education Act was specifically designed to teach black citizens only the very basic skills they would need to work for white people. Trains and buses were segregated. Public beaches were segregated, with the best ones reserved for white citizens. Pedestrian beaches, drive-in movie parking spaces, parks, pedestrian crossings, taxis, and even graveyards were segregated.

Those in favor of apartheid argued that once apartheid had been fully implemented, black people would no longer be citizens in their own country of South Africa. Instead, they would become citizens of the so-called independent "homelands." When this happened, black South Africans would become "foreign" guest laborers who merely worked in South Africa as the holders of temporary work permits.

A man shows his government passbook, identity documents whose possession was required by all black and Coloured South Africans during apartheid. The passbooks were required for employment and travel within the country, among other things. When the requirement of the documents was first established, hundreds of South Africans burned their passbooks in an act of defiance against the government.

It is important to note that not everyone either supported apartheid or silently went along with it. A substantial white minority stood in opposition to the apartheid government as well. Organizations such as the Black Sash and the largely white (but legally banned) South African Communist Party worked in opposition to the apartheid government. During the 1970s and 1980s, between 15 percent and 20 percent of white voters voted for the liberal Progressive Party. But for many years its Member of Parliament (MP), Helen Suzman, provided the only parliamentary opposition to apartheid.

South African Jews, although only accounting for 2.5 percent of South Africa's white population and 0.3 percent of South Africa's total population, played a large role in the anti-apartheid movement. For example, when 156 political leaders were arrested in December 5, 1956, more than half of the whites arrested were Jewish.

Not only was there internal opposition to the apartheid government, there was international opposition as well. As early as 1962, the UN General Assembly passed Resolution 1761, which condemned South African apartheid policies. On August 7, 1963, the UN Security Council established a voluntary arms embargo against South Africa, which was made mandatory in 1977 after the Soweto Uprising.

The South African government, though, did not care about opposition, either internal or external. They were convinced that apartheid was both morally correct and politically necessary for the Afrikaners to maintain their way of life and dominance in South Africa.

Under apartheid, white minority domination of the black majority was absolute. But although black citizens were powerless, they were not silent. In the darkest days of apartheid, the African National Congress made itself heard.

THE ANC

The first thing to remember is that the black citizens of South Africa are not just one ethnic group—they are composed of many tribes, subtribes, and peoples. For black South Africans to have any chance to stand up to the white establishment, their first priority would be to come together and reach a unified common ground.

In 1911, South African Pixle ka Isaka Seme, along with several other young African leaders who had recently returned from studying in England, called on Africans to forget their differences and unite together under one organization. He said (as quoted on the Web site of the African National Congress), "We are one people, these divisions, these jealousies, are the cause of our woes today."

So on January 8, 1912, tribal chiefs, representatives of social and church organizations, as well as other prominent individuals, gathered together in Bloemfontein to form the South African Native National Congress. This group was later renamed the African National Congress.

In some of its earliest actions, the ANC led a campaign in Transvaal against the much-hated passes, which controlled black Africans' movements, ensuring they worked either in the gold and diamond mines or on the farms. The ANC also supported a militant strike by black mineworkers in 1920.

Some ANC leaders disagreed with militant actions such as strikes and protests. They argued that the ANC should achieve its aims through persuasion rather than action.

This moderate approach meant that the ANC was not very active in the 1920s. Other organizations, such as the Industrial and Commercial Workers Union (ICU), were more active and militant. This group did win some victories for its workers, but it could not sustain itself; in the late 1920s it collapsed.

Socialist organizations also began to organize black workers in the 1920s. The International Socialist League along with other Socialist organizations formed the Communist Party of South Africa in 1921. Although originally a white organization with slogans such as "Workers of the world, unite and unite for a white South Africa," the party changed in 1924. In that year, the Communist Party became the first nonracial political organization in South Africa, and they worked toward organizing black workers and "Africanizing" the party. Because of this, many blacks joined the communists, seeing in them a political party that promised fair wages and an end to racial inequality.

Despite the growth of the Communist Party, the ANC exploded with new life and energy in the 1940s. It was at that time that it began changing from the careful organization it was in the 1930s into the mass movement it was to become in the 1950s.

Increased attacks on the rights of black people, along with the rise of extreme Afrikaner nationalism in the 1940s, created a need for an angrier, more militant response from the ANC. Harsher racism also brought greater cooperation between the organizations of Africans, Coloureds, and Indians. In 1947, the ANC and the Indian Congresses signed a pact stating full support for each other's organizations.

Perhaps most importantly, in 1944, the ANC Youth League was formed. The young leaders of the Youth League—among them Nelson Mandela, Walter Sisulu, and Oliver Tambo—based their ideas on African nationalism. They fervently believed that Africans would only be freed through their own efforts. The Youth League aimed to involve the masses—as many people as possible—in militant struggles against the white establishment.

The ANC Youth League Manifesto of 1944 stated their case quite eloquently:

> South Africa has a complex problem. Stated briefly it is: The contact of the White race with the Black has resulted in the emergence of a set of conflicting living conditions and outlooks on life which seriously hamper South Africa's progress to nationhood.
>
> The White race, possessing superior military strength and at present having superior organizing skill has arrogated to itself the ownership of the land and invested itself with

The ANC's Youth League, formed in 1944 with the idea that Africans would be freed only through their own efforts, spawned such leaders as Walter Sisulu *(left)*, Nelson Mandela *(center)*, and Harrison Motlana *(right)*, who are photographed at the Defiance Campaign trial at the Johannesburg Supreme Court in 1952. It was this group that would inspire Thabo Mbeki.

authority and the right to regard South Africa as a White man's country. This has meant that the African, who owned the land before the advent of the Whites, has been deprived of all security which may guarantee him an independent pursuit of destiny or ensure his leading a free and unhampered life. He has been defeated in the field of battle but refuses to accept this as meaning that he must be oppressed, just to enable the White man to further dominate him.

The African regards Civilisation as the common heritage of all Mankind and claims as full a right to make his contribution to its advancement and to live free as any White South African: further, he claims the right to all sources and agencies to enjoy rights and fulfill duties which will place him on a footing of equality with every other South African racial group.

The majority of White men regard it as the destiny of the White race to dominate the man of colour. The harshness of their domination, however, is rousing in the African feelings of hatred of everything that bars his way to full and free citizenship and these feelings can no longer be suppressed.

This, then, was the world of South Africa in the 1940s. A government determined to keep black citizens and white citizens as separate as possible. A government determined to make black South Africans noncitizens in their own land. A government determined that black people would live in a state of total and perpetual inferiority to white people.

But it was also a time when the African National Congress was beginning to make its voice heard. And it, too, was determined, determined to bring about an end to apartheid and bring freedom and equality to the black majority. It was into this world that Thabo Mbeki was born in the year 1942.

4

Childhood

THABO MBEKI WAS BORN TO GOVAN MBEKI AND EPAINETTE MOERANE on June 18, 1942, in a small village in the Transkei called Mbewuleni. (The name means "a place of seed.") His parents' involvement in politics virtually guaranteed that Thabo was born to follow in their footsteps.

His mother Epainette (today known by her clan name of Ma Mofokeng) was the child of a lay preacher in the Methodist Church. Her family was from the elite Bafokeng clan. Her father owned a dairy farm, as well as wheat and sorghum fields. Education was important to the family. All seven of his children received educations, an extraordinary achievement for a black family in South Africa at that time. After receiving a Cape senior certificate (the highest school diploma available to blacks at the time) Epainette became a teacher. She found a position at the Taylor Street Elementary School in Durban, where she taught English and geography.

While at Taylor Street Elementary, she met Betty du Toit, an Afrikaner woman and a member of the Communist Party of South Africa. Under her influence, Ma Mofokeng joined the party as well, although today she is no longer a member.

It was also at Taylor Street Elementary that Ma Mofokeng met her future husband, Govan Mbeki. He too came from a religious family—his father was such a devout Methodist that he would say grace even before drinking a glass of water.

The family was of the Mfengu or Fingoes clans. Members of these clans were typically well educated and affluent and produced many of the region's teachers, preachers, shopkeepers, and public servants. The Mbeki family was no exception. Nearly all of Govan's older siblings became teachers. Govan, too, initially went in that direction.

During the late 1920s, Govan traveled throughout the Transkei with his cousin Robert. Robert was an organizer for the Industrial and Commercial Workers Union (ICU). Through his travels, Govan became acutely aware of the hardships that black South Africans lived with on a daily basis, and vowed to do whatever he could to help improve their lives.

Others influenced him as well. Through Eddie Roux and his wife, Win, he learned about communism, and of their dream of revolution against tyranny and oppression. His closest friend was Thabo Mofutsanyana, who was known as Edwin. (White South African officials often gave black citizens Western names, which were easier for them to pronounce.) Govan and Edwin would spend hours talking about political theory and ideology. They were so close that when Govan's first son was born, he named him Thabo after his best friend.

But when Govan and Ma Mofokeng began dating, it wasn't all talk of politics and the future. Govan was an excellent rugby player, and Ma Mofokeng loved watching him play. The couple also loved ballroom dancing, and many of their happiest hours were spent on the ballroom floor, tangoing and fox-trotting. Years later, in his prison writings, Govan noted that while in solitary confinement on Robben Island, he would rehearse those steps in his cell and imagine his wife smiling in his arms.

One day in 1938, Govan received a telegram from the Clarkesbury Institute, a teaching-training college in his Transkei homeland, offering him a job. Govan jumped at the chance to return home. But, taking this job caused the first of many periods of separation between him and Ma Mofokeng. The couple managed to see each other during school holidays, and, finally, in 1940, they married.

Govan had already begun to supplement his teaching income by writing. He had published a book, *Transkei in the Making*. This led to an offer to edit a newspaper, the *Territorial Magazine*. He was also appointed director of the *Guardian*, a weekly journal.

After losing his teaching position at Clarkesbury, he and Ma Mofokeng decided to remain in the Transkei. They moved to a tiny village called Mbewuleni, near Idutywa. The village is a tiny isolated settlement of only about three dozen kraals, or family homesteads.

Initially, the Mbeki kraal consisted of two mud, thatched huts: one for Govan and Ma Mofokeng, and another one for cooking. When the children were born, a third hut was added.

By Mbewuleni standards, the family was fairly well off. Govan had some income from his political writings. In addition, when settling in Mbewuleni, the couple had opened a small general store, called the Goodwill Store. It was an all-purpose general store that sold things that people in the village couldn't grow for themselves—things like tea, sugar, chocolate, and soap. Not only that, the shop was also the village post office, so, in no time, it became the center of town life.

Ma Mofokeng supplemented the family income by baking cakes and rolls for a local coffee shop. Govan did his part as well by doing typing and clerical work, such as for the local Cattle Dipping Committee.

The couple's first child, Linda, was born in 1941. As quoted in *The Life and Times of Thabo Mbeki* by Adrian Hadland and Jovial Rantao, Govan said, "Then I remember chatting, my wife and I. Enough of girls. Why? Because boys remain in the family all their lives and girls have a habit of leaving the family and adopting new names. Also, if anything goes wrong with girls, they become the burden of other families."

The next year, Thabo was born. As Govan is quoted as saying in *The Life and Times of Thabo Mbeki*, "He was, according to my wish, a boy. But between my wife and I, there was an arrangement. She was Sotho-speaking, I'm Xhosa-speaking, and we said all children must have both Xhosa and Sotho names. So I had a great friend, Thabo Mofutsanyana, or Edwin, and I named Thabo after him. Like me, Thabo's Xhosa name, Mvuyelwa (He for whom people sing), never stuck." The family grew further with the additions of Thabo's two younger brothers, Moeletsi, born in 1945, and Jama, the youngest, in 1948.

Thabo had a fairly typical childhood. Friends describe him as "playful" and quiet. As his classmate Sonwabo Gustavus Mphahlwa remembered him (as quoted in *The Life and Times of Thabo Mbeki*), "Thabo never spoke much. He was also very clever. We played a little cricket and 'jump-jump.' We also took part in athletics but our favorite was relay. I was good at that and so was Thabo."

Thabo attended Ewing Primary School, which was just across the valley from the Mbeki kraal. It was a one-room school, nothing more than a tin shed with two mud huts alongside for the principal and for cooking the day's meals. The principal, Jeffrey Mphahlwa, was known for being a strict taskmaster.

"When we were late [for school] he used to punish us by administering corporal punishment. He would hit our hands with a branch. It was painful," remembered Sonwabo Mphahlwa. Thabo, though, was nearly always on time.

Thabo Mbeki's parents, pictured here in 1987, taught him the importance of education, commitment, and political activism.

But even though Ewing Primary was run in a very strict manner, there was the occasional break. Fridays were dedicated to music, and all the local schools in the district took turns hosting music concerts. It was a great time for Thabo to meet the other children in the area, and he enjoyed the singing and dancing.

Also, once a week the government truck arrived, bringing food and supplies for both the school and Ma Mofokeng's shop. Classes came to a stop while the students rushed to unload packages of bread, peanut butter, raisins, and jam for the school. While they were doing that, Thabo and his younger brother Moeletsi would load up the sledge with the supplies for the store.

Pulling the sledge was the task of the family's mule, Dyakopu. Dyakopu was renowned throughout the valley for his meanness and stubbornness. As quoted in *The Life and Times of Thabo Mbeki*, schoolmate Mickey Nama remembered Dyakopu well. "If you went in front, it would try and bite you. If you went behind, it would kick. Thabo was the only one that Dyakopu would go quietly with."

As anyone who has ever lived in the country or in a small village knows, life quickly falls into a routine. After school, Thabo would walk home with his brothers and sister to the family kraal across the valley. Once there, he would wash his clothes with water brought from the well by Dyakopu and then hang them out to dry.

After that, he would clean out the suitcase, really just a wooden soapbox, in which he kept his clothes. Each of the Mbeki children had their own box, and Ma Mofokeng insisted that they each keep their boxes clean. After the box was clean, and all his other chores were completed, young Thabo would iron his own clothes and pack them away in the suitcase.

As his sister Linda remembered, (quoted in *The Life and Times of Thabo Mbeki*), "Ma always kept us busy. She likes to see children busy all the time." Ma agreed, "We expect our children to be handy at home. Thabo did what the others did. If there were dishes to be washed, he was there."

LOVE OF READING

While Thabo's life was fairly typical of any black South African youth, in one crucial aspect it was very different: This was that Thabo loved nothing more than reading. He would read while he was walking to and from school. He would read while he was working in the family shop. He would read any spare moment he had at home. On some days, he would stay in the hut he shared with his brothers and sister and read all day!

As his father, Govan, remembered, (quoted in *The Life and Times of Thabo Mbeki*),

> Thabo has always been a great reader. He read a lot of books at home, including my first one (*Transkei in the Making*) which was published in 1939 on the Transkei. There were all sorts of books there, Marxist-Leninist, the Communist Manifesto. They were there and he read them all and other literary ones, and so on. My wife used to complain about him. 'I don't like Thabo, he's just like you,' she would say. 'He never does anything with his hands. Moeletsi helps around the house, Thabo doesn't. He just reads books.'

Of course, Ma's words were words said in anger. Thabo certainly did his share of work around the house and in the shop. But still, he would sit down and read anytime he could avoid chores.

But there was one academic subject Thabo initially did poorly in—math. And, like kids all over the world, he did what he could do avoid the subject. Every morning, Thabo would say he had a stomachache and stay in bed. Then, as the day went on, and it was too late to go to school, he would start to feel better and get up and start reading. Ma Mofokeng realized that something was wrong, and she contacted the school's principal, who told her that Thabo was having problems with math.

Since she had only stopped teaching a few years before, Ma took matters into her own hands. "The next morning, as usual, he had a stomach ache in the morning," she is quoted as saying, in *The Life and Times of Thabo Mbeki*. I asked somebody to bring me a piece of chalk from the school and I started him in mathematics from scratch. I drew on the ground and

THABO FELT A STRONG CONNECTION WITH THE AMAQABA. HE'D EVEN PUT DOWN WHATEVER HE WAS READING TO TALK WHENEVER ONE CAME INTO THE SHOP.

used objects: 'If I have this many cattle outside the kraal, and bring these in, how many are in the kraal?'" Thabo quickly caught on, and his daily stomachaches came to an end.

WORKING IN THE SHOP

Like his brothers and sister, Thabo was often called upon to watch the family shop. But unlike his siblings, he felt most comfortable and talkative with the members of his community known as the "red people," or the amaqaba. When one of them entered the store, Thabo always put down the book he was reading and spoke to them with kindness and respect.

There were, in fact, two kinds of people living in Mbewuleni. The amaqaba, or "red people," were by far the majority. The "red people" had never been to school and did not know how to read or write. Instead of Western-style clothes, they wore blankets. Instead of Christianity, they believed in the traditional African gods. They were very poor, and they were called "red people" because they rubbed ochre, a red mud, all over their faces and bodies.

The other kind of people was the amakholwa. Known as the "educated ones," they had been to school, dressed in Western clothes, were Christians, and had some money. Although the Mbeki family was amakholwa itself, Thabo felt a strong connection with the amaqaba. He'd even put down whatever he was reading to talk whenever one came into the shop.

Ma Mofokeng, as quoted in *They Fought for Freedom: Thabo Mbeki*, laughed at the memory. "Thabo was always at his best with the red people. He talked to them for hours and hours. If another person came to the house or to the store, he would close up. If a red person came, he would even forget he was reading." Thabo was always interested in hearing the problems of the "red people" and would do whatever he could do to help.

Like any general store in a small isolated village, Ma Mofokeng's Goodwill Store was more than just a store. It was also a place for advice, for medical surgery, for pharmaceuticals, just about anything one could think of.

And because he could read well, Thabo was often called upon to read the villagers' letters out loud to them. Many of the men of the community worked in the mines in Johannesburg, and, with no phone service in Mbewuleni, they relied on letters to stay in touch with their families. Of course, if the families could not read, they'd have to ask Thabo to read the letters for them.

Providing this service quickly introduced Thabo to a world of adult problems. As Govan remembered in an interview with Bridget Thompson for the documentary *Heart and Stone*, "Every store is some sort of postal agency and we had our own postal bag. There was a high rate of illiteracy in one section of the population . . . and you have got to read their letters. Often they would open the letter in the shop and they would get hold of my own children: 'Here, come read here.' Or write the letter in reply . . . those children got to hear about things at an age when they should not have heard about it. There's a husband working away from his family and he writes his wife at home and the husband has heard reports . . . 'oh, your wife is doing this and the other thing.' Then the husband takes the women to task in the letter. And the children read it. But, well, it's a service that had to be done."

There were other ways that enabled young Thabo to enter the world of adults. His father, Govan, was still actively involved in politics: reading, writing, attending political meetings, even

THE ADULTS ASKED HIM QUESTIONS ABOUT HIS VIEWS, AND HE WAS EXPECTED TO BE ABLE TO BACK THEM UP WITH FACTS AND LOGIC, JUST LIKE AN ADULT.

serving on local boards. Many evenings, friends of Govan and Ma would come to the family's house. There, they would sit late into the night, talking about politics and the situation in South Africa.

Although he was still young, Thabo took part in the discussions as well. The adults asked him questions about his views, and he was expected to be able to back them up with facts and logic, just like an adult. Thabo quickly proved his worth and was soon able to hold his own in discussions with anyone. His intelligence was so respected that he was asked by a neighboring chief to give advice on the government's new cattle policy. Not bad for a young village boy only 12 years old!

This is not to say that these occasions happened every night. The family was simply too busy to spend much time relaxing. Thabo's mother was always busy: running the shop, cooking, baking, cleaning, and helping other residents of the village. Govan himself hated being disturbed while reading or writing, and he was frequently away on trips.

"I never really had time for the children," he said in the documentary *Heart and Stone*. "Not that I didn't love them. But I was doing writing and reading so I didn't have the time to be playing with them. So I pushed them to the mother, 'Come go and play there or get to your mother or leave me alone.' So that I don't know how they feel today. Probably they feel that I didn't pay sufficient attention to them as children. I wouldn't blame them if they felt like that. Now even when

I get my grandchildren . . . I can't be with them for long. I'm doing something and I want to be left alone."

Even though Thabo's family was relatively well-to-do by local standards, life was still difficult. Although the family earned income from odd jobs, Govan's occasional journalism, and the Goodwill Store, there was often not enough money for even the essentials of life. As Govan said in the documentary *Heart and Stone*, "We didn't have much . . . we were so poor that for underpants, my wife had to use my pants because we couldn't afford to buy her any."

The situation became even worse in 1953 when a fire broke out in the store and kraal, destroying many of the family's possessions. Then, to top everything off, a storm hit Mbewuleni, causing even more destruction.

Govan was forced to stop working part-time and return to teaching. However, there were no teaching jobs in their own village, so he had to leave his family behind in search of work, finally finding a teaching position in the distant town of Ladysmith. He was never really to return home.

Thabo, too, had to leave home. Ewing Primary School only went up to standard four (grade six). In order to continue his education, he was sent to a school in Queenstown. His sister, Linda, left home at the same time, entering a convent at Ngcobo. Ma Mofokeng was left behind to take care of the shop and the remaining children.

The family never really reunited under one roof. Thabo was forced to become even more independent and self-reliant. But while we may consider a family forced to live apart as something unnatural, Thabo saw it differently. As quoted in *The Life and Times of Thabo Mbeki*, he said, "By the time we grew up, we were used to being without our parents. We didn't feel the separation; it was a condition of life."

With the move to Queenstown, Thabo entered into a new stage of his life. Although only 10 when he left home, he was more mature than most boys his age. And his level of political awareness, already high due to his parents' interests, was about to grow even greater.

5

Political
Education

IN QUEENSTOWN, THABO LIVED WITH HIS UNCLE, MICHAEL MOERANE.
Michael was Ma Mofokeng's brother and a music teacher.
While evenings at the Mbeki house had been filled with political discussions, evenings at the Moerane home were filled with music. Michael had six children (Kabeli was Thabo's best friend), and each of them played a musical instrument. In the evenings, they would all play their instruments, accompanied by Michael on the piano.

Even Thabo got into the act. One night, Govan came to visit his son and was pleased at what he found. As quoted in *The Life and Times of Thabo Mbeki*, "One evening I got to Queenstown, to my brother-in-law's house and I find him sitting at the piano and each of his six children has his or her own music instrument and he is accompanying them. Thabo is playing the flute and would play the piano too. That was very good. Almost every evening that's what my brother-in-law did with his family."

But while Thabo spent his time studying, reading, and playing music, he did not forget his political beliefs. Events were about to take place that would lead to his first overtly political act.

In 1951, the Defiance Campaign against Unjust Laws was presented by the ANC at a conference held in Bloemfontein, South Africa, in December 1951. Based on noncooperation with laws they considered to be unjust and discriminatory, the ANC decided to take action the following year. If, for example, black citizens were not allowed on a certain train, they would break the law and get on the train. If they were not allowed on a particular bridge, they would use that bridge. This would be the first time organized resistance was planned against the apartheid regime. Because of this, the ANC issued a lengthy public statement that said, in part,

> All people, irrespective of the national group they belong to and irrespective of the colour of their skin, who have made South Africa their home, are entitled to live a full and free life.
>
> Full democratic rights with direct say in the affairs of the government are the inalienable right of every South African —a right which must be realized now if South Africa is to be saved from social chaos and and tyranny and from the evils arising out of the existing denial of the franchise of vast masses of the population on the grounds of race and color.
>
> The struggle which the national organizations of the non-European people are conducting is not directed against any race or national group. It is against the unjust laws which keep in perpetual subjection and misery vast sections of the population. It is for the creation of conditions which will restore human dignity, equality and freedom to every South African.

ANC supporters gather in Johannesburg in 1952 to protest racial segregation in South Africa. Although Thabo Mbeki was too young to partake in the demonstrations, he began to discuss politics and organize committees among his friends.

Demonstrations in support of the Defiance Principles were organized for April 6, 1952. This date was the 300th anniversary of white settlement in the Cape of Southern Africa. In Queenstown, Thabo had heard about the upcoming demonstrations. One day, an ANC convoy drove past his uncle's house, calling on all residents to attend a meeting the next day. Thabo and his cousin Kabeli decided that it was time for them to join the party and actively become part of the campaign.

But to join the ANC, Thabo and Kabeli would need money for membership dues. So the next day, Thabo and Kabeli snuck out of the house to collect empty soda bottles. After hours of work, they finally gathered up 24 bottles, which they turned in to a local shopkeeper, who redeemed them for the two shillings and sixpence they needed to join.

The boys quickly rushed off to the meeting, eager to become full-fledged members of the African National Congress. Imagine their disappointment when they were told they were too young to join the party! Although they were sad that they were not able to join, they knew that it was only a matter of time before they'd be old enough.

While Thabo was temporarily thwarted in his drive to get more directly involved in the politics of the day, his father, Govan, was busier than ever. He had been fired from his teaching position in Ladysmith because of his political beliefs. Govan then moved to Port Elizabeth, where he became the local editor and office manager of the newspaper *New Age*. Thabo would take the train down to Port Elizabeth whenever he could to visit his father.

WORSENING TIMES

Even when visiting his father in Port Elizabeth, Thabo didn't get to spend as much time with him as he might have liked. Since the National Party had taken power in 1948, new laws had been enacted that touched every aspect of both Govan's and Thabo's lives. And because of the new laws, Govan spent even more time teaching young people about politics and what they could do to help change the system.

Because of the Group Areas Act, Thabo could only live in township or homeland areas, not wherever he wanted to live. Because of the Suppression of Communism Act, his parents' political beliefs were now illegal. Because of the Separate Amenities Act, Thabo was not allowed to swim in the local swimming pool or to use the public library. Because of the Bantu Education Act, Thabo could only receive enough education to perform manual labor. And finally, meetings of more than 10 black citizens were soon to become illegal as well. A noose was tightening around the entire black community.

So while Govan was giving political education classes to new ANC recruits, Thabo began his own efforts at organization. As Hadland and Rantao point out in their book, *The Life and Times of Thabo Mbeki*, "He . . . began to discuss political matters with his friends just as his father was doing. While other children of his age were going to the movies or playing in the park, Thabo's friends established committees. The restrictions on the number of black people who could gather in the same place meant, once more, that there was no room for Thabo at his father's side. Only this time, it was enforced by the police and the punishment for any infraction was arrest and imprisonment."

But despite his work as a political organizer, Thabo was still just a kid in school. At school in Queenstown, he studied hard, got As on his tests, and earned the respect of both his fellow students and his teachers. He was, by most accounts, a brilliant student.

After two years in Queenstown, Thabo switched schools again. This time, he moved to a school in Butterworth, in the Transkei. This was much closer to his home village of Mbewuleni, which allowed him to see more of his mother, as well as his younger brothers.

Again, Thabo excelled in school. He received his junior certificate with a first-class pass, and he and his parents decided

Even sporting arenas were segregated under the apartheid regime. In this 1969 photograph, people of color are sectioned off from white fans, even if only by a few inches.

that he would now go to Lovedale College, in Alice. Although he was only 14, he started directly into the matric program. (This is the program that would lead him, if he did well, to university studies.)

Lovedale had been started by missionaries in 1824. Many of South Africa's future leaders, including Thabo's own father, had been educated there. It was at Lovedale that Thabo became increasingly more involved in student politics.

In 1955, he joined the Society of Young Africans and then the school branch of the ANC Youth League in 1956. When the government passed the Bantu Education Act, the Youth League at Lovedale took prompt action, and a strike was called. Serving on the executive committee, Thabo was deeply involved in the strike's organization. This brought him to the attention of many influential people in the ANC. It also brought him to the attention of the school administration, which promptly expelled Thabo from Lovedale.

Thabo arrived back home at Mbewuleni in 1959. Govan bought him a full set of the subjects he needed from a correspondence school and told him to get to work completing his matric. Thabo, though not happy at being back in his tiny home village, got to work at once. Although studying was his top priority, he was just 16 years old, and he found it easy to find a distraction from his schoolwork. Her name was Olive Nokwanda Mphahlwa. She was, in fact, the daughter of the famously strict principal at Ewing Primary School, Jeffrey Mphahlwa. The couple began meeting in secret, and soon Olive became pregnant.

While not completely unheard of, sexual relations outside of marriage were still a relatively rare event. Dating itself really didn't exist in tiny rural South African villages—courtships were set up that led directly to marriage. A pregnant underage girl caused quite a stir.

Since Govan was living in Port Elizabeth, it was up to Ma Mofokeng to deal with Olive's angry parents. Thabo was only

16, so it was determined that he would have to pay the usual penalty for making an underage girl pregnant—five head of cattle. As Ma Mofokeng said, quoted in *The Life and Times of Thabo Mbeki*, "The girl's family was cross, but what could they do? I was not happy myself either."

Thabo's only child, Kwanda Monwabise, was born in 1959. He lived with his mother and her family for 10 years. After that, he moved in to the Mbeki kraal and was raised by Ma Mofokeng until he passed his matric. His mother, Olive Nokwanda, became a nurse and currently lives in Port Elizabeth.

Thabo had other distractions from his studies as well. On March 21, 1960, South African police killed 69 and wounded over 180 black protestors at Sharpeville. The protestors, unarmed, were demanding to be arrested for refusing to carry their passbooks. In apartheid Africa, any demonstration by black South Africans was taken as a provocative act and more than likely to bring about a violent response from the white authorities. As Lieutenant Colonel Pienaar said in later questioning, "The Native mentality does not allow them to gather for a peaceful demonstration. For them to gather means violence."

The shootings set off a wave of black protests, followed by a major crackdown by South African security forces. The government declared a state of emergency and arrested more than 18,000 people, including Thabo's father, Govan.

Worried about his father, and concerned over the welfare of his son, Thabo earned only a second-class pass on his matric exams. Even so, he was eager to continue his studies. He knew, though, that there was nowhere in the Transkei, or anywhere in the Eastern Cape, that had the schools he needed. Once again, he would have to leave his home, this time for South Africa's largest city, Johannesburg.

There he would stay with a well-known attorney from Soweto and take courses at Britzius College. Excitingly for

Sharpeville was the site of a 1960 massacre, in which black South Africans were wounded and killed. Police opened fire on a group of unarmed demonstrators protesting the rule that forced black South Africans to carry passbooks to travel within their own country. Following the event, Govan Mbeki was arrested by the government.

Thabo, almost as soon as he arrived in Johannesburg, he got to meet Nelson Mandela.

As Thabo described it in an interview with the *Star*, "I met Nelson Mandela for the first time in 1961. I had traveled from the Eastern Cape to Johannesburg and on my arrival received a message that he wanted to see me. I was taken aback that Mandela wanted to see me. He invited me to his house in Orlando West for lunch. We sat and chatted for a long time about a whole lot of issues, about the problems in the ANC Youth League and the youth movements in general. At that point I was active in the ANC Youth League. When I recollect that meeting, I realize how our discussion illustrated Mandela's ability to be in touch with developments on the ground. To date I do not know how Mandela knew that I was in town."

Thabo Mbeki, who had spent his life in villages and smaller towns, with relatively easy access to either his mother or father, was now on his own in the big city. At first, he was overwhelmed by the noise, the crime, the constant harassment by the police. But he soon settled into a life of political meetings and studies. And, just like his mother with Betty du Toit, he found a white mentor who was eager to help him succeed.

Anne Welsh was his teacher at Britzius College who helped run the South African Committee for Higher Education. She immediately recognized Thabo's intelligence and drive, and so she decided to do whatever she could do to help him on his way. She also knew that despite his academic achievements, the apartheid educational system would never allow him to reach his full potential.

But even though Thabo was fully committed to his education, politics were never far away. He was asked by the leadership of the ANC to start a new political group called the African Students' Organization (ASO). As the ASO's organizing secretary, Thabo traveled throughout South Africa, talking to other students about the African National Congress and its goals of equality and liberation.

On May 31, 1961, South Africa declared itself a republic, cutting its last bond with the British Empire. One of its first moves as a republic was to declare the ANC an "unlawful organization." Govan Mbeki, who had already served five months in prison following the Sharpeville Massacre crackdown, was once again arrested for "furthering the aims" of the now illegal ANC.

Despite the turmoil surrounding him, Thabo received almost straight first-class passes. He was particularly praised for the quality of his writing: natural, logical, and often lyrical. His political work and the high quality of his studies made it clear to the older generation of ANC leaders that Mbeki was one of their great hopes for the future.

After finishing his post-matric studies, Thabo began working on his bachelor of arts in economics by correspondence with the University of London. But Anne Welsh, his former teacher, had something else in mind for him. She wrote a letter to Thabo's parents. As quoted in *the Life and Times of Thabo Mbeki,* "Your son has a gift. I have written to the University of Sussex in Britain recommending him for a scholarship to study for a Masters in Economics. If you can see to him getting there, I will see to his fees."

Anne Welsh knew that if Thabo remained in South Africa his future would be bleak, with nothing more to look forward to than arrest or death at the hands of police. She knew that for him to have a future in South Africa, he would, at least temporarily, have to leave the country.

6

Exile

THE TIME WAS RIGHT FOR THABO MBEKI TO LEAVE THE COUNTRY BECAUSE events were taking a violent turn. For years, the ANC had tried by every peaceful means possible to convince the government that every citizen of South Africa, whatever his race or color, should have the right to vote. But now, with the government banning the ANC altogether, a new form of resistance was begun.

Leaders of the ANC became convinced that the South African government was incapable of listening to reason. So, in an act of desperate defiance, the ANC formed a military wing, called Umkhonto we Sizwe (meaning "the spear of the Nation"). Perhaps, the logic went, they would listen to arms.

Govan Mbeki was one of the group's founding members and a part of its high command. In Port Elizabeth, he created a unit designed to perform acts of sabotage. He knew that now was the best time for Thabo to leave the country. There were two problems, though. One was that, like his father, Thabo had no travel documents that would allow him to leave the country legally. The second problem was the knowledge that if Thabo did leave the country illegally, he would be unable to return until liberation.

The leadership of the ANC knew that, as with other student leaders, Thabo's life was in danger as long as he was in South Africa. Government security forces were arresting anyone they thought was fighting to overthrow the whites-only regime. Some of those arrested were tortured, some were killed. ANC leaders decided that for their own safety, the future leaders of South Africa would have to leave the country and go to school abroad. There, safely out of the country, they would be able to get the education they and their country would need for them to succeed as leaders. When apartheid ended, they would be brought back home.

Because Thabo was lacking the proper papers, he would be unable to leave South Africa by plane. He would have to go by land, crossing the South African border into any neighboring country by foot. Once out of the country, he would then have to make his way to Tanzania and meet up with a group of ANC sympathizers. It was decided that he should try to enter into Botswana (then called Bechuanaland) and go from there to Tanzania.

Before he and the other group of students went into exile, they received a summons from Nelson Mandela. Despite the fact that he was living underground and on the run from the police, he insisted on having a farewell face-to-face meeting with Thabo and his friends.

Thabo described the meeting in an interview with the *Star* in April 1996, "We met him at a secret venue in Mayfair where he conveyed his best wishes to the group and issued his last instruction before our departure. As part of our final instruction, he made two points to us. The first was that we were ambassadors of South Africa abroad and that we needed to behave properly. Secondly, he said that as one of the first groups of ANC students leaving to study abroad there was an immense responsibility on us to succeed. He said that when the struggle against apartheid was over we would be expected to play a leading role in the processes of reconstruction of a post-apartheid South Africa. What struck me about this meeting was that Mandela was underground, under a lot of pressure evading the police, but still found the time to meet with this group, wish them well and boost their morale. To reach Mandela, we took all sorts of routes before we finally got to him. When we met him he was in disguise. What struck me during meetings in 1961 and 1962 was that despite all the pressure he was under, [he] had a genuine concern for ordinary people. He risked his life to come and bid farewell to ordinary members of the ANC."

In September 1961, Thabo and 30 other students began their journey into exile. Among the group were several who would become leaders in the future, postapartheid South Africa. Manto Tshabalala-Msimang would become Nelson Mandela's deputy minister of justice and later Thabo Mbeki's controversial minister of health. Simon Makana would go on to become South Africa's ambassador to Russia.

Leaving Johannesburg, Thabo and the others felt a combination of excitement, fear, and sadness. None of them knew whether they would be able to return to their native country. They were all leaving their families and lives behind them, not knowing when, or even if, they would ever be able to come home again.

Thabo was leaving behind his parents, his sister and brothers, his girlfriend, and his son. His father, Govan, had recently been arrested for the third time, acquitted, and placed under house arrest. His younger brothers were in school in Lesotho. His sister, Linda, was in Cape Town taking business classes. Ma Mofokeng was all alone, left behind to take care of the family shop and kraal. The family was now completely split up.

ESCAPE

The group had a cover story ready in case they were stopped by the police: They were a football (soccer) club and its supporters on their way to a match in Botswana. The group had been driving for hours when they reached a police roadblock. The police had known they were coming and were looking for Thabo.

He was arrested and taken to the Zeerust Magistrates Court where he was charged with not having a reference book (the "passport" needed by black citizens to travel within South Africa). The others in the group, now leaderless, were sent back to Johannesburg.

Thabo was fortunate that he had lived with the advocate (attorney) Duma Nokwe. From him, Thabo knew that the law allowed him to ask for additional time to present his reference book to the proper authorities. The judge freed him, giving him just 48 hours to return to Johannesburg and take his book to the nearest police station.

Upon returning to Johannesburg, Thabo rejoined his friends, ready to flee the country immediately. They decided that it was too dangerous for them to drive on the main highway, so they took smaller dirt roads, which made the trip last much longer.

Finally, they made it safely into Botswana, where they met a group of ZANU freedom fighters who led them by foot across the border into southern Zimbabwe (then Southern Rhodesia). But when they reached the town of Bulawayo, they were arrested again for not having travel documents. This time, they were kept in jail for six weeks.

The group was terrified. They were told that they would be sent back to South Africa, where they all faced certain arrest. Fortunately for Thabo and the others, a friendly court clerk, Cyril Ndebele (who would go on to become Zimbabwe's parliamentary speaker), gave him some helpful advice.

When they appeared before the judge, Thabo argued that they should not be returned to South Africa. The law, he said, stated that they must be sent back to the country where they came from. And since they had entered Zimbabwe from Botswana, *that* was the country that they should be sent back to.

The judge agreed, and they were sent back across the border to Zimbabwe. Once there, they were met by ANC representatives who took them to the airport in Botswana, provided them with travel documents, and put them all on a plane to the city of Dar es Salaam in Tanzania (formerly Tanganyika). Finally, the group was safely out of South Africa.

Unfortunately for Thabo, it took several more weeks before his flight to Britain could be arranged. The university term in Britain had already started, and every day he remained in Dar es Salaam meant another day further behind in his classes. It was November before he finally arrived in Britain.

Upon arriving in London, he immediately contacted the University of Sussex, where he was supposed to have begun his studies in September. He was told that he was too late for classes this year and would have to reregister the following year.

Once again, Anne Welsh came to the rescue. She contacted the university and begged them to allow Thabo to register. Explaining the extraordinary circumstances that led to his delay, she argued that with his superior intellect and drive he would have no problem catching up with his classes. University officials agreed, and Thabo left London for Essex, ready and eager to begin his studies.

LIFE IN EXILE

At the age of 21, Thabo Mbeki was free for the first time in his life. He could argue and debate anyone freely without the fear of being arrested. He could read books that had been banned in South Africa. He could walk into any restaurant, any bar, any library, anywhere he wanted. He could become friends with anyone of any race, and walk the streets without carrying his identity papers.

Back home in South Africa, though, things were going from bad to worse. Many activists had been arrested, there was unrest throughout the nation, and security forces were doing whatever they could do to destroy any movements for freedom. It is estimated that by 1964, the ANC had only three or four active members left in South Africa and less than a hundred sympathizers. The vast majority of the organization was now working in exile.

While many southern African nations had become home to small groups of ANC members, London became the unofficial headquarters of the ANC in exile. Once again, Thabo was in just the right place at the right time, doing work that would get him noticed by the leadership of the ANC.

He quickly began building the youth and student sections of the ANC in exile, traveling around the world telling people about apartheid. His work caught the notice of Oliver Tambo, the president of the ANC, who then lived in London. Oliver, or OR as he was called (his name was Oliver Reginald), invited Thabo and a few of his friends to visit him.

As Tambo's wife, Adelaide, recalled (quoted in *The Life and Times of Thabo Mbeki*), "A group of six or seven young ANC students came round to our house in Highgate one day. Oliver gave them all assignments and asked them to report back the following day. When they came back the next day, some had done half the job, and the others had done nothing. Only Thabo had done all he was required to do. Oliver was angry with the others. They had all been asked at the same time, given assignments at the same time, and some had not produced. Thabo had done perfectly everything he was required to do. Oliver said to me, 'There are a lot of leadership qualities in that young man.'"

After this, Oliver and Adelaide Tambo became like second parents to Thabo, an exile in England whose parents were far away in South Africa. They had him visit them often, and encouraged him in his studies and his political work.

Oliver Tambo *(above)* was president of the ANC and became Thabo Mbeki's mentor in England, picking up where Govan Mbeki left off. Tambo was a powerful force against apartheid, traveling around the free world to speak against the regime and recruiting students for the ANC.

Thabo took his politics and his studies very seriously. This is not to say, of course, that Thabo was all work and no play. He enjoyed talking with friends about things other than politics, walking the streets of London, and listening to jazz and blues music. He loved poetry, and he even wrote a thesis on the poetry of Shelley and Keats!

THE RIVONIA TRIAL

In July 1963, Thabo learned that his father, along with many other top ANC officials, including Nelson Mandela, had been arrested at Liliesleaf Farm in the Johannesburg suburb of Rivonia. They were charged with high treason, a charge that carried with it the death penalty.

At the trial, under threat of death, Nelson Mandela made one of his most famous speeches,

> During my lifetime I have dedicated myself to the struggle of the African people. I have fought against white domination, and I have fought against black domination. I have cherished the ideal of a democratic and free society in which all persons live together in harmony and with equal opportunities. It is an ideal which I hope to live for and achieve. But, if needs be, it is an ideal for which I am prepared to die.

Imagine how helpless Thabo must have felt, living in exile in Essex, unable to speak to his father. But unable to sit around and do nothing, Thabo led a protest march from Sussex to London and persuaded the British government to plead for mercy.

His efforts worked. Govan Mbeki, Nelson Mandela, and the rest of the Rivonia defendants were spared death and sentenced to life imprisonment. They were sent to prison on Robben Island and were not seen by the public for almost 30 years.

FINISHING HIS EDUCATION

Although Thabo knew the importance of completing his education, he still felt trapped and helpless in Sussex. He wanted

RE BANNINGS EXPECTED

...e between the Government's ...th Africa's resistance move-

...d claim that Poqo has been ...ear and the Communist under-...re "mopping up" the remainder.

● Mr. V. Mini, member of the Port Elizabeth SACTU committee, and secretary of the Metal Workers' Union.

● Mr. L. Mancoko, also of Port Elizabeth, and secretary of the General Workers' Union.

● Mr. E. Loza, chairman of the Cape Town SACTU Branch, and

See also pages 5 and 24

secretary of the Commercial and Distributive Workers' Union.

● Mr. K. Ndlovu, of Durban, secretary of the Railways Workers' Union; and

● Miss L. Kazi, secretary of the African Food and Canning Workers' Union.

The SACTU spokesman told POST this week that the organisation had written a letter to the International Labour Organisation in Geneva. The letter said that "discriminatory laws and the removal from office of democratically elected union officials by banning, confining orders and 90-days' detention without trial, cut deeply across ILO principles."

He described allegations that SACTU is a political body and that it is affiliated to the Communist World Federation of Trade Unions as "smears."

Matter of time

Mike Norton reports from Cape Town that politicos in the Cape — even those considered "moderate"— are expecting to be arrested at any moment, following the detention of Dr. Neville Alexander (see page 24), who is described as a "political lamb" by his associates.

Many of them have already made what provision they can for their families "when we go to prison"—so sure are they that they will be picked up.

"It is only a matter of time," said one. "My whole life has been devoted to the search for a non-violent solution of the problems of this country. But . . ."

He predicted that "thousands" of arrests on a nation-wide scale would follow the Rivonia swoop. Minister of Justice Vorster was saying at the same time: "I do not expect large-scale, country-wide arrests."

About 50 prominent people in the Peninsula alone have been banned— or have fled the country.

Among them are Barney Desai, Reggie September, Brian and Sonia Bunting, Jan Hoogendyk (house arrested), Alex La Guma (90 days), Cardiff Marney and now Dr. Neville Alexander.

Teachers

The Teachers' League of South Africa has been hard hit—with ten of their Peninsula members banned and three dismissed from their jobs.

The Coloured People's Congress have had eight banned, two of whom have fled — and one jailed and one detained.

SACTU offices in the Cape have suffered repeated raids.

Three Liberal Party members have been banned and one warned in the Cape; eight Congress of Democrats members have been banned; anti-CAD have had three banned; and 17 Africans of various political opinions in the Cape have been banned.

A CPC spokesman said there was a possibility that the CPC would be banned following the Johannesburg swoop.

Congress

Although the Indian Congress movement in the Republic has not been banished as an organisation, it has been damaged by a spate of bannings within the last seven weeks.

Its leadership has been silenced and few men who have made a name for themselves in the Congress movement remain at the head of affairs.

In a statement to POST in Durban, members of the Congress said: "It is obvious that the 'gag' orders are meant to silence, stifle and paralyse Congress: We are a peaceful body and have held the banner of non-violence.

"A total of 60 years of banning has been imposed on 12 persons."

● CONTINUED ON P. 24

Port Elizabeth shocked by police swoops

POST Reporter — Port Elizabeth

RESIDENTS in Port Elizabeth were startled last week to hear of the police swoop in Johannesburg on former African National Congress leaders — two of whom were from Port Elizabeth.

The two local men — Govan Mbeki and Raymond Mpokamisi Mhlaba — have been away from their homes in New Brighton for a long time. Mbeki disappeared about a year ago and Mhlaba left in 1961.

They are now being held with 15 others, including Walter Sisulu and Ahmed Kathrada, under the 90-day clause.

GOVAN MBEKI

Mbeki — former school teacher, trader and well-known journalist, is a graduate of Fort Hare where he studied for his B.A. at the same time as Chief Kaiser Matanzima.

During the 1960 Emergency, Mbeki was detained with other New Brighton political leaders. He was later charged with members of the Continuation Committee but was acquitted on appeal.

Last year he was acquitted after being charged with three others under the Explosives Act.

Mbeki's wife lives at Idutywa. Their eldest son is studying at London University. Another son is at Roma College, Basutoland. The third child, a daughter, is a stenographer in Cape Town.

Mhlaba is a former student of Healdtown Institution. A popular speaker at New Brighton in the heydays of the banned ANC, he was a member of the provincial executive.

He slipped out of the country in 1961 shortly after his wife was killed in a road accident.

This newspaper from July 21, 1963, records the arrest of Govan Mbeki in an article entitled "Port Elizabeth Shocked by Police Swoops." Miles away from his home country, Thabo worried about his father, who had been charged with high treason for speaking out against the government. However, living in a free country worked to his benefit: Thabo was able to persuade the British government to intervene on his father's behalf.

to do more to help in the liberation of South Africa and was eager to take part in the armed struggle against apartheid. On two separate occasions, he asked Oliver Tambo for permission to quit school and join the ANC's military wing, the Umkhonto we Sizwe. Both times, Oliver Tambo refused to allow Thabo to quit school. He understood how important it would be for Mbeki to finish his education before taking up arms against the apartheid regime.

Thabo was disappointed in Tambo's decision, but he dove into his work at the university with determination. He was certain that when he graduated, his life would be devoted to the liberation of South Africa. Still, at times despair set in, as he contemplated the immensity of the task ahead of him.

In 1966, Thabo received his master's degree in economics. At this time, he received, for the first and last time, a letter from his father in prison. In it, Govan urged Thabo to continue his education and to work on getting his doctorate. Govan felt that the doctorate would open up new opportunities for his son. Thabo, though, had had enough with schooling.

LONDON

Instead, he went to work full-time in the ANC's London office for Oliver Tambo and Communist Party leader Yusef Dadoo. But while Thabo had stopped his formal schooling, his real education was just about to begin.

It was while working in London that Mbeki learned the ins and outs of working for a political organization. Inside South Africa, the ANC had been largely destroyed. The organization in London was split into different factions or groups, each with its own idea about how to proceed. Since Mbeki had the obvious support of ANC President Oliver Tambo, people knew that he was both somebody to watch as well as somebody to be wary of. With Tambo's support, he could become a threat to their own positions.

Because he had so many potential enemies within the organization, Mbeki quickly realized the importance of surrounding himself with political allies, people who would watch his back and loyally support him. During his years in Sussex, he had organized and become friends with many young South African exiles. These people, including his brother, Moeletsi, became his most trusted advisors. While many of them were not even close to being his intellectual equal, they were people he could rely on and trust.

As Hadland and Rantao point out in their biography, *The Life and Times of Thabo Mbeki,* at this stage of his life, most of the elements of his persona were in place. He was bookish and studious. But unlike most others of a scholarly bent, he also had an ability to get along with people—a skill developed during his years of political organizing. From the time he worked in his mother's store, he had exhibited an understanding and consideration for the poor. In addition, he had a gift for taking the long view of things (rather than looking for a quick fix) and an appreciation for having loyal allies surrounding him.

He was also, as Hadland and Rantao point out, despite everything in his personal life, lucky. He had always been in the right place at the right time—at the center of political activity. He had been lucky enough to get out of South Africa when he did. And, fortunately for Mbeki, his luck was to continue.

During his time in London, he reconnected with Zanele Dlamini, a social worker studying for her postgraduate degree at the University of London. Zanele grew up in the Alexandra township of Johannesburg with her five sisters and one brother. Zanele had originally thought of becoming a nurse, but instead she received a bachelor's degree in social work at the University of Witwatersrand in Johannesburg. While there, she was active in student politics, and it was then, she says, that she first met Thabo when he was an organizer for the African Student's Organization. (Mbeki, however, doesn't remember anything about that first meeting.)

Nelson Mandela lived for nearly 30 years in this prison cell on Robben Island. Mandela became the most famous of the imprisoned ANC leaders and was the international face of the antiapartheid movement.

This time, the two quickly fell in love, but it was soon to be a long-distance relationship. For although Mbeki's credentials as an ANC leader were excellent, he was still the recipient of some criticism. Some questioned that while he had been a longtime member of the Communist Party, he had been educated solely in the West. These members of the ANC, who had received their training in East Germany or in the Soviet Union, felt that he was not sufficiently radical and lacked the necessary military training to truly be a strong leader.

Since the 1969 ANC consultative conference had reaffirmed the movement's dedication to armed struggle, Mbeki realized that to be considered a legitimate leader within the ANC, he would need military training. This time, when he submitted his application it was okayed, and he was soon on his way to Moscow.

TRAINING IN THE SOVIET UNION

It was 1969 when Mbeki arrived in Moscow for a year's study at the Institute of Social Sciences. The next year, Max Sisulu, the son of ANC leader Walter Sisulu, reached Moscow, and the two of them set out for military camp in the remote town of Sekhodvia.

It was, perhaps, the most difficult year of Mbeki's life. He had always been a scholar; nothing could possibly have prepared him for the tough physical training, the marching and drilling, and the loneliness and isolation that he endured that cold Russian winter.

He and Max had been assigned to an officer's military training course. One night, the South African group, led by Mbeki, was sent off on a training exercise. They spent hours marching in the frigid weather, going from one marker to the next. Mbeki was the platoon leader and carried the only map. Deep into the exercise, the group began to feel lost, and Mbeki, about to consult the map, discovered that it, too, was lost!

After searching the immediate area, it became clear that the map had been dropped somewhere along the march. The platoon was forced to retrace its steps until eventually the map was found and the exercise could be finished. Mbeki's friend Max recounted the incident in *The Life and Times of Thabo Mbeki*, "Nobody was pleased, we were exhausted. I could never imagine Thabo as General Thabo. I could see him then as a political leader, but not as a military one."

Despite such setbacks, Mbeki persevered and completed his military training. While in the Soviet Union, the only person he communicated with was Zanele. But it was impossible for him to write to her directly. He would send his letters to Zanele to Dr. Yusuf Dadoo at his office at the South African Communist Party in London. Dr. Dadoo would then bring the letters personally to Zanele. She in turn would keep the Tambos and the rest of Mbeki's friends informed as to his progress.

After finishing his training, Mbeki returned to London, his critics silenced, his military and political credentials earned. He was immediately promoted and sent to Lusaka in the country of Zambia. There, he was to be the assistant secretary to the Revolutionary Council. This newly formed council, led by Oliver Tambo, would quickly become the center of ANC and South African Communist Party (SACP) activities. Once again, Thabo Mbeki's luck had sent him to the heart of the action.

7

Action

BY THE EARLY 1970S, THE CENTER OF ANC ACTION HAD SHIFTED TO southern Africa. Prisoners newly released from South African jails who immediately left the country, along with others already in exile, set up ANC structures in the countries surrounding South Africa: Swaziland, Lesotho, Botswana, Angola, and Mozambique. This closer access to South Africa allowed easier communications and transfer of weapons to those still within the country.

Mbeki, working closely with ANC president Oliver Tambo, began receiving positions of greater and greater importance. One of his first assignments was to go to Swaziland to become the acting head of the ANC mission there. One of his main tasks was to brief new exiles and to help build up the ANC's structure. It was here that his ability to listen and communicate proved invaluable.

Sometimes, though, he took a more active role. The ANC was attempting to train and send guerillas into South Africa. For that, they would need weapons and ammunition. Mbeki would drive to the Mozambican border at night, returning back through Swaziland with a carload of weapons. This was a dangerous assignment, since both the South African military and the Swaziland police were on the lookout for him.

Mbeki also began giving political and military training to South African students who had fled from South Africa. He would then send them on to ANC camps in Mozambique and Zambia for additional training. In this way, he built up a personal network of ANC cells and agents. He also served as a middleman, putting ANC members in touch with each other, and helping them to form small groups.

At the same time, other political movements were starting up in South Africa. The Black Consciousness Movement and the South African Students Organization, led by Steven Biko, attracted many new younger members. In order for the ANC to remain at the forefront of the fight against apartheid, Thabo had to work to bring these new groups into the ANC. Because of his tireless work, these groups gradually became affiliated with the ANC, making the ANC even more powerful.

MARRIAGE

While Mbeki was based in Lusaka, Zanele was in the United States, working on her doctorate. The couple met whenever they could. Thabo would send a telegram to Zanele, letting her know when he was going to be in London. She would then fly over to meet him. The two gradually fell even more in love and decided that they wanted to marry.

Getting married, though, was not as easy as it sounded. The ANC had strict rules when it came to marriage. Since ANC members were living in exile and without money, it was the party that paid for weddings and gave the couple their

Due to his murder while in police custody, Stephen Biko (1946–1977) became a martyr for his cause, the Black Consciousness Movement. Passionate that blacks should not settle for being a part of South African society, Biko fought for the restructuring of South Africa around the black majority. A best-selling book and a movie about his fight brought about international awareness of South Africa's oppressive regime.

rings. Because of this, the marriage of ANC members had to be approved by a committee.

As Adelaide Tambo said in *The Life and Times of Thabo Mbeki,* "The custom was in the ANC that people didn't just go and get married. They must get permission from the organization. . . . Sometimes the leadership would say, 'no, you didn't come here to get married,' or, 'no, you have been marked for another assignment and can't get married now.'"

Thabo, now 32 years old, was terrified that his application for marriage would not be approved. He told Adelaide Tambo (quoted in *The Life and Times of Thabo Mbeki*), "Mama, if Papa [Oliver Tambo] doesn't allow me to marry Zanele, I'll never, ever marry again. And I'll never ask again. I love only one person and there is only one person I want to make my life with, and that is Zanele." Fortunately for all concerned, permission was granted for the marriage of Thabo Mbeki and Zanele Dlamini.

The couple was married on November 23, 1974, at a registry office north of London. A small party followed at the home of Oliver and Adelaide Tambo. The official celebration, though, was held, somewhat surprisingly, at the country manor of Lady Edith Glanville-Grey.

Lady Glanville-Grey was, in fact, Zanele's sister. She had been working as a nurse in Zambia where she met the man she would marry, Lord Glanville-Grey, the cousin of Queen Elizabeth. Lady Glanville-Grey insisted that Thabo and Zanele celebrate their marriage at her Farnham, Hampshire estate.

There were more than 300 people in attendance, including many members of the British aristocracy—lords, ladies, earls, and dukes—not a typical ANC marriage by a long shot (although the ANC did still provide the rings).

At the party, telegrams were read from around the world, congratulating the happy couple. Telegrams were received from both Govan Mbeki (still in prison) and Ma Mofokeng.

Thabo Mbeki and Zanele Dlamini began their ANC-approved marriage in 1974. Highly educated and politically conscious in her own right, Zanele is a gender activist working toward the empowerment of women in South Africa.

The Tambos had asked Ma Mofokeng, as was the custom, to provide Zanele with her Sotho clan name, welcoming her to the family. The name chosen was Ma Motlalekhotso, meaning "one who brings peace."

BACK TO WORK

After the marriage, Zanele went back to the United States to complete her doctorate. Upon receiving it, she went to work for the UN High Commissioner for Refugees. Working for the United Nations, she was able to travel easily, and soon she moved to Lusaka to be with her husband.

Returning to Swaziland, Mbeki immediately went back to work. His generation of exiles had spent years out of Africa receiving military training in Cuba, East Germany, and the Soviet Union. When these exiles returned to Africa, they often found themselves set apart from their communities, and easily picked up by local police. Mbeki set to work training them in basic explosives, weapons, and grenade skills; then he sent them to South Africa with a list of personal contacts to continue building up the ANC underground network.

By the time of the Soweto Uprising in 1976, this network had helped tens of thousands of students who left the country and wanted to fight against apartheid. Thabo Mbeki's long work in setting up cells, groups, and networks of ANC members was beginning to show results.

Soon, Mbeki himself would have to find a new location to set up his base of operations. In early 1976, the government of Swaziland signed an agreement with the South African government vowing that the ANC would not be allowed to move weapons or cadres from Swaziland into South Africa. Mbeki was asked to leave the country, and returned to Lusaka, Zambia.

He was becoming an important ANC leader. He was elected to the party's highest body, the national executive committee. And, in December 1976, he was assigned the job of ANC's chief representative in Nigeria. He and Zanele left Lusaka for a new life in Lagos.

MBEKI DID EVERYTHING HE COULD TO LEARN THE FATES OF HIS BROTHER AND HIS SON.

TRAGEDY

In Nigeria, one of Mbeki's jobs was to assist young South Africans in settling into their lives in exile and beginning their studies in universities throughout Nigeria. He also traveled a great deal, meeting ANC members and many African politicians, and, as always, working to help bring democracy to South Africa.

While in Lagos, Mbeki learned some tragic news. His youngest brother, Jama, had gone missing. A member of the ANC, it was suspected that the police had killed Jama, but his body was never found. Further bad news followed when Thabo's only son, Kwanda, also went missing. Once again, it was suspected that the police had killed him, but his body, too, was never found.

Mbeki did everything he could to learn the fates of his brother and his son. After the end of apartheid, the Truth and Reconciliation Committee (TRC) was established to help discover the truth of what happened during the horrible years of apartheid. Even the TRC, though, was unable to learn the fates of Jama and Kwanda.

Despite his personal grief and loss, Mbeki continued in his work. He spent the next years in Nigeria and also traveled the world, speaking out against apartheid. He helped convince the United Nations to declare apartheid a "crime against humanity" and urged it to impose economic sanctions against South Africa. This would mean that no country would be allowed to sell anything to South Africa and would not be allowed to purchase South African products. Many felt that this sort of economic pressure would help convince the South African government to abandon apartheid and to bring democracy to the country.

AMERICAN AND BRITISH REACTIONS

Although most Western nations took a strong position against the apartheid government, both the United States and Britain were more ambivalent. Margaret Thatcher, then the British prime minister, called the ANC a terrorist organization. In 1987 she said that anyone who believed the ANC would ever form the government of South Africa was "living in cloud cuckoo land."

Both Prime Minister Thatcher and then U.S. president Ronald Reagan saw South Africa as a nation holding strong against the forces of communism. Since the ANC was supported by the South African Communist Party, they were convinced that the ANC itself was a communist organization, and unworthy of support. It would be better, in their view, to have a repressive white minority government than a possibly communist black majority government.

President Reagan vetoed a bill that called for limited economic sanctions against the South African government. Instead of speaking out or taking action against apartheid, the Reagan administration began a policy of what they called "constructive negotiation" with the South African government. For many observers, "constructive negotiation" meant doing nothing at all to end apartheid, while giving tacit approval to the South African government.

The Reagan administration turned out to be on the wrong side of history. As Nobel Peace Prize-winner Desmond Tutu said while testifying to Congress, "In my view, the Reagan administration's support and collaboration with it [apartheid] is equally immoral, evil and totally un-Christian. . . . You are either for or against apartheid and not by rhetoric. You are either in favor of evil or you are in favor of good. You are either on the side of the oppressed or on the side of the oppressor. You can't be neutral." Nelson Mandela was ultimately given the U.S. Presidential Medal of Freedom in 2002.

Also during this period, a struggle was taking place within the ANC itself. Many important officials, such as Chris Hani and Joe Slovo, believed that armed struggle was the only way to liberate South Africa. Others, led by Oliver Tambo and Thabo Mbeki, worked hard to persuade the ANC that discussions and negotiations might work. After all, they reasoned, years of armed resistance had brought no results.

Mbeki began a series of secret meetings with influential Afrikaner teachers and businesspeople. He knew that it would be necessary to persuade them that they had nothing to fear from a democratic South Africa. A black majority government would not seek revenge against the white minority.

In 1978, after three years in Nigeria, Mbeki was called back to ANC headquarters in Lusaka. He was appointed Oliver Tambo's political secretary and then director of information. In these positions, he had more influence on the ANC's direction and plans.

While in favor of negotiations, Mbeki never gave up on his calls for action. He called for a campaign to make South Africa "ungovernable." Between September 1984 and April 1985, the homes of 814 police officers were destroyed or made uninhabitable. Hundreds of township councilors resigned, responding to demands that they do so. In some ways, the apartheid state was being torn apart from within.

Nelson Mandela, still in prison on Robben Island, pleaded time and time again for South Africa's prime minister, P.W. Botha, to speak with the ANC. Botha, though, refused. He even declared a state of emergency in 1985, in response to the renewed violence, giving the police and the army extraordinary powers.

In 1986, the government even made an attempt on Thabo Mbeki's life. A captain in the South African Defense Force was

Thabo Mbeki quickly exhibited his value to the ANC and began a dramatic ascent up the organization's ladder. In this 1986 photograph, as ANC director of publicity and information, Mbeki works at his desk in Zambia.

sent to Lusaka, ordered to place a bomb in Mbeki's house. But before he had a chance to carry out his plot, he was arrested by the Zambian police.

In 1987, Govan Mbeki was released from prison due to poor health. He was 79 years old. Upon his release, Govan settled in Port Elizabeth (his wife was in Idutywa) and soon traveled to Lusaka to meet with the ANC leadership in exile to discuss the ongoing talks.

Meanwhile, protests and marches against the government became more and more widespread in South Africa. Unions went on strike, and every day people were being killed in greater and greater numbers. Businessmen within South Africa, afraid of the spreading turmoil, urged the government to speak with the ANC. Governments outside South Africa also urged Botha to begin negotiations. Finally, even Botha himself came to the realization that it was time to talk with the ANC. The country was rapidly becoming ungovernable, and if negotiations didn't start soon, the country would easily end up in a full-blown civil war.

SECRET TALKS

The year 1988 saw both sides in a stalemate. The South African government was coming to the realization that force would not work to quell the unrest. The leaders of the ANC were reaching the conclusion that violence alone would not and could not bring an end to the apartheid government. Both the ANC and the South African government began looking for a way to begin negotiations.

In 1989, Thabo Mbeki lobbied other African governments to adopt the Harare Declaration. This declaration, issued on August 21, 1989, called on the South African government to release all political prisoners, lift the ban on restricted organizations such as the ANC, remove troops from the townships, and end the state of emergency. When those conditions had been met, negotiations could begin. Later that year, Mbeki led an ANC delegation to New York, where the UN General Assembly, along with the Security Council, adopted the resolution as well. The ball was now in the court of the South African government.

Cautiously, slowly, talks began. Secret channels were set up to allow Mandela to consult with the ANC in Lusaka. President P.W. Botha had met with Mandela personally. It was decided that members of the National Intelligence Service (NIS) would be the ones within the government to make direct contact with the ANC.

The question was with whom would they speak? Although many were convinced that Mbeki should be the one, others were not as sure. Some in the ANC leadership worried that if the talks failed Mbeki himself would get the blame. If that happened, it could jeopardize his position in any future majority government.

They felt that Mbeki was destined to become president, and didn't want him to do anything that might harm his future chances. Indeed, some now feel that an agreement had been made as early as the 1970s that when apartheid ended, Mbeki would eventually be president of South Africa. In her book *Anatomy of a Miracle,* Patti Waldmeir argues that an agreement to make Thabo Mbeki president was made between Nelson Mandela and Govan Mbeki while Thabo was still herding goats in Mbewuleni!

But despite the obvious political risks, most knew that Mbeki was the ideal person for the job. The NIS felt that he was the obvious choice as well. But the delicate question still remained on how exactly to set up the meeting. Thus began Operation Flair.

The meeting would take place in Lucerne, Switzerland. Switzerland was chosen as the site because it was the only country other than Great Britain that allowed South African citizens to visit without having a visa. It was also thought that it would be easier to hold the meetings in Switzerland, undetected.

Secrecy was important. Few in either the ANC leadership or in the South African government knew about the meeting.

Mike Louw and Maritz Spaarwater were the representatives of the NIS. Thabo Mbeki and Jacob Zuma represented the ANC. The political stakes for the ANC were extraordinarily high: Was the meeting a trap of some sort? Both parties knew that if the talks failed, South Africa would destroy itself in a civil war.

When the meeting began, tensions were high, so Mbeki decided to break the ice with a joke. As quoted in *The Life and Times of Thabo Mbeki*, he walked up to Louw and Spaarwater and said, "Well here we are, terrorists, and, for all you know, communists too." All four of the men laughed, breaking the obvious tension.

As the talks began, the relationship between Mbeki and Louw grew stronger as they learned they had several things in common: among them a love of poetry and an appreciation of whiskey, in particular, Johnny Walker Black Label. The two men, representing two opposing forces, were able to establish a relationship based on respect and trust.

After that first meeting in Lucerne, both sides were able to report success. Upon returning to Lusaka, Thabo telephoned Nelson Mandela in prison, informing him of the South African government's willingness to negotiate. Similarly, Louw and Spaarwater were able to inform the government that the ANC was willing to negotiate as well.

President P.W. Botha had become ill just prior to the meeting, and F.W. de Klerk became the new state president and leader of the National Party. The meeting had been so secret that even de Klerk hadn't been informed, and he was surprised when Louw and Spaarwater returned from Switzerland to brief him about the meeting's success!

Preliminary talks continued. And, in a gesture of goodwill, President de Klerk released several top ANC leaders from prison in 1989. When Walter Sisulu and other released leaders

In 1987, Govan Mbeki was finally released from Robben Island. At 79, he was South Africa's oldest political prisoner. Winnie Mandela, wife of ANC leader Nelson Mandela, stands by Mbeki's side upon his arrival in Johannesburg on November 7, 1987. Govan Mbeki died in 2001.

got off the plane in Lusaka they were met by 32 members of the ANC's National Executive Committee.

And, after a separation of more than 20 years, Govan Mbeki was reunited with his oldest son, Thabo. Obviously, in that time

Thabo had grown from a teenager to a man. He now had a beard, smoked a pipe, and was married. He had also become one of the ANC's most important leaders. Instead of a big emotional reunion between the father and his son, the two shook hands, just like any other comrades. Obviously, their time apart had diminished any emotional connection the two might once have had. As Govan recalled the moment, quoted in *The Life and Times of Thabo Mbeki*, "I saw Thabo again at the end of 1989 after more than 20 years. We met in Lusaka. I don't know if I had any special feelings, but I was pleased to see him."

EVERYTHING CHANGES

On February 2, 1990, South African president F.W. de Klerk addressed the National Assembly in Cape Town. In a surprise speech, which has become known as the "unbanning" speech, President de Klerk announced that he would repeal discriminatory laws and lift the bans on the ANC, the South African Communist Party, and other liberation movements. He also ordered the release of all political prisoners. The National Assembly and the people of South Africa were shocked and surprised by his sudden move.

It was the beginning of a new era in South Africa. On February 11, Nelson Mandela was released from prison after 27 years of incarceration. And for the ANC leadership in exile, it was now time to return home.

8

Return to South Africa

ON APRIL 27, 1990, THABO MBEKI, ALONG WITH MEMBERS OF THE ANC leadership, boarded a plane for South Africa. He had been in exile, away from his home and family for 28 years.

When the ANC members looked out the window of the plane as they crossed the Limpopo River into South Africa, a feeling of excitement passed over the group. "We all stood up and stared out of the window," recalled Thabo, in an interview with the *Sunday Star*. "There was a lot of excitement building up as we were moving further south. There was a lot of happiness that people were coming back. But there was also some sadness that it was ever necessary that we should be outside the country for so long.

"Why didn't the Government . . . realize the futility of the apartheid system? But then life in exile has in a way been rewarding. . . .What has sustained everybody is that nobody spent a life of idleness. People learned something. The other

ANC members and supporters of Nelson Mandela await his arrival in Soweto on February 13, 1990.

thing that sustained them is that they never lost confidence that one day the apartheid system will go and that one day they will return home and everybody would have played a role in the process. There is really no bitterness against the people who caused all this suffering. The bitterness is really against the system and not against the people."

Even though Mbeki had played a crucial role in making the ANC's return to South Africa, there were still some in the party who disagreed with his diplomatic approach. These people, including militant leaders such as Joe Slovo and Chris Hani, still felt that only an armed struggle against the government would bring freedom to South African blacks. They felt that the ANC should not even be negotiating with the government, which they saw as "the enemy." They worried that Mbeki would give away far too much and make too many concessions in return for democracy.

Mbeki didn't worry too much about their concerns. He knew that there was still a lot of work to do before an agreement could be reached that allowed elections in which every South African, regardless of race, would be allowed to vote.

On May 2, 1990, a meeting took place at the official house of South Africa's prime minister, Groote Schuur. In attendance were members of the National Party government; Nelson Mandela, leading the group that had been imprisoned on Robben Island; Archie Gumede, leading activists who had been working inside South Africa; and Thabo Mbeki, leading the ANC delegation that had been in exile. It was, to say the least, a historic event.

As Mbeki said after the meeting and the signing of the Groote Schuur Accord, (quoted in *The Life and Times of Thabo Mbeki*), "We were all of us a bit surprised . . . within a matter of minutes, everyone understood that there was no one in the room with horns—and, in fact this discussion ought to have taken place years ago. And when we closed, the general feeling was that not only was forward movement necessary, but that it was also possible."

POWER STRUGGLES

In July 1991, for the first time since the 1960s, the full membership of the ANC was able to meet in conference. At that conference, Mbeki urged the ANC to officially end its policy of armed struggle against the apartheid government. Although many members felt that the ANC should not give up its policy until the South African government was defeated, Mbeki convinced the majority of members that the time for armed resistance was over.

It was also at this conference that a struggle began over who would lead the party. Oliver Tambo, who had been president of the ANC since 1969, was ill and ready to step down. Nelson Mandela, who had been the deputy president, was elected as the ANC's new leader. This left the post of deputy president open.

Many, including the members of the ANC Youth League, felt that Thabo Mbeki was the logical choice for the position. The more militant members, though, felt that Chris Hani should have the job. It looked as if it would become a major political fight between Mbeki and his allies favoring negotiations, with Chris Hani and his allies still supporting armed struggle.

The party leaders, including Nelson Mandela, did not want a fight that could split the party. Both Mbeki and Hani were asked to withdraw from the election, and a compromise candidate, Walter Sisulu, was made deputy president instead. Two years later, Chris Hani was killed by a right-wing gunman, and the political rivalry between Hani and Thabo came to an end.

At the same 1990 conference, another political rival of Mbeki's, Cyril Ramaphosa, was appointed to be the lead negotiator in talks with the government. Ramaphosa had joined the ANC underground in 1986. He was a well-known trade-union organizer, and was the head of South Africa's largest trade union, the National Union of Mineworkers. He later became the secretary general of the Congress of South African Trade Unions (COSATU), the nation's biggest union federation.

The extent of the political rivalry between Thabo Mbeki and Cyril Ramaphosa is open to some debate. As lead negotiator and ANC secretary general, many felt that Ramaphosa was the natural choice to be Mandela's deputy president after elections were finally set. But when Mbeki was ultimately appointed to

On May 4, 1990, South Africa's president F.W. de Klerk *(left)* met with ANC president Nelson Mandela to discuss relations between the South African government and the ANC.

that position, many felt that it reflected Mbeki's ruthlessness in defeating political adversaries. Others felt, though, that he was always Mandela's first choice, and that Ramaphosa was never really in consideration for the job.

During the next few years of negotiations, the two political rivals both played important roles. As Dullah Omar said, quoted in *The Life and Times of Thabo Mbeki,* "Thabo was the great thinker and strategist. He was the one we would go to to obtain final direction. Cyril was the implementer, the negotiator. Cyril and Thabo's roles were complementary. There was no conflict between them at all. They worked together." Still, during these years, at least in the public's eye, Mbeki was definitely taking a backseat to Ramaphosa.

Behind the scenes, Mbeki played a crucial role in persuading both the white right wing and the Zulus to join in the negotiations. The right wing was led by General Constand Viljoen, the former head of the South African Defense Force. He had an army of 60,000 troops and was prepared to fight to obtain a piece of South Africa in which only white people could live and work. They called this their "Volkstaat."

Mbeki and the ANC were committed to keeping South Africa a whole nation, where each citizen's rights would be protected. After careful discussions, it was decided that a clause would be added to the interim Constitution, promising the right to self-determination and group rights for all. This satisfied the right-wing Afrikaners, and they decided not to fight.

Mbeki also met with the leader of the Inkatha Freedom Party (IFP), Mangosuthu Buthelezi. Mbeki had been instrumental in helping Buthelezi start the IFP back in the 1970s. Now, he helped to convince Buthelezi to join the election and not continue fighting.

With this successful pair of negotiations, Mbeki, despite being temporarily pushed aside within the ANC leadership by Cyril Ramaphosa, played a critical role in bringing about a peaceful progression toward a democratic South Africa. If the right wing and the Zulus had not been convinced to give up their arms, an all-out civil war could still have easily taken place. Working behind the scenes, Mbeki helped to make sure that that did not occur.

DEMOCRACY

After years of careful negotiations under the auspices of the Convention for a Democratic South Africa, a draft constitution was approved on July 26, 1993. It allowed for a federal system of regional legislatures, equal voting rights regardless of race, and a bicameral (two-part) legislature.

Cyril Ramaphosa *(right)* was the secretary general of the ANC and Thabo Mbeki's political rival. Here, he is shown greeting conservative Afrikaner-Volksune Andries Beyers in Johannesburg in 1993.

On April 27, 1994, for the first time in the nation's history, elections were held in which every South African over the age of 18, black or white, could vote. It was a glorious day. Thabo Mbeki's dream of a nation where all citizens were equal had become a reality. South Africa was now a free and democratic country.

As expected, the ANC won the election with more than 62 percent of the vote. As head of the party, Nelson Mandela was to become the nation's first black, democratically elected president. Despite the prominent role played by Cyril Ramaphosa, Mandela named Thabo Mbeki to be his deputy president. To this day, nobody is certain what led Mandela to reject Ramaphosa for Mbeki.

In any case, for Nelson Mandela and Thabo Mbeki, taking power was just the beginning. Now, they had to work to rebuild a nation nearly destroyed by years of oppression and unrest.

9

Rebuilding
a Nation

WHEN THABO MBEKI ARRIVED AT HIS NEW OFFICES ON HIS FIRST DAY AS deputy president of South Africa, he was in for a shock. The previous occupants had stripped the office nearly bare. There were no telephones, no rugs, and no computer. All that remained was a dusty desk and an old swivel chair. Undaunted, Thabo sat himself in the chair, rolled up his sleeves, and set himself to work.

There was much to be done. The new government had to get rid of the laws that regulated apartheid and replace them with new ones. A new constitution had to be put in place.

The problems at times seemed nearly insurmountable. In 1994, 2.3 million South Africans did not have enough food on a daily basis. Thirty percent of the population could neither read nor write. In Gauteng, South Africa's financial center, 25 percent of all black people lived in substandard housing, in houses little better than shacks. Unemployment was widespread. Education and medical care were nearly nonexistent. In essence, the nation would have to be rebuilt.

Over the next five years, Mbeki worked tirelessly as deputy president. He traveled the world meeting with other leaders, informing them about the transformation taking place in South Africa. At home, he worked hard to implement the policies needed to bring about change in South Africa.

In 1996, Mbeki introduced the Growth, Employment, and Redistribution (GEAR) economic policy. This ambitious program was devised to stimulate South Africa's economy to 6 percent growth by the year 2000, as well as to create 500,000 new jobs. The policy was widely praised by both the South African and the international business communities.

Mbeki also worked hard to make the government more workable. He brought Responsibility for Youth Affairs, the disabled, the status of women, the Central Economic Advisory office, and the Government Communication and Information Service together under the leadership of the deputy president. While this consolidation may have made the government more effective, some of Mbeki's critics felt that it was nothing more than an attempt to build up his own power.

As the months and years passed, Mandela slowly ceded more and more responsibilities to his deputy president. At times, this led to an awkward relationship between the two men. While Mandela was getting older, he often resented that his authority was being lessened.

For Thabo, it was sometimes difficult working under the shadow of Nelson Mandela. Mandela, after all, was a worldwide icon and hero, the symbol of the new South Africa. He knew that he was always going to be compared to Mandela, and that there was little chance that he could come out ahead against a man revered as a near saint.

Despite the occasional tensions between the two, it became clear that Thabo Mbeki would become South Africa's next president. In December 1994 he was elected deputy

Thabo Mbeki and Nelson Mandela appear together on June 16, 1999, the day of Mbeki's inauguration. Mandela waves as he prepares to leave the office of president in the capable hands of his ANC colleague Mbeki.

president of the ANC. And then, finally, in 1997, he was elected as the ANC president. With that, Nelson Mandela, while still president of South Africa, had become a figurehead leader, a symbol of change in South Africa. The real power belonged to Thabo Mbeki. Thus, it was no surprise to anyone that Thabo Mbeki was elected as president in the 1999 elections, winning a two-thirds majority in the parliament. No longer a figure in the background, Mbeki was now the man in charge.

10

President

SINCE BECOMING PRESIDENT, THABO MBEKI HAS EMERGED FROM THE shadow of Nelson Mandela to become a powerful and influential leader in South Africa and throughout Africa. He has made South Africa a regional power broker, and has promoted the idea that African political conflicts should be solved by Africans.

In order to do this, he headed the formation of both the New Partnership for Africa's Development (NEPAD) and the African Union (AU). Mbeki hopes that structures like these will help to make Africa less dependent on foreign aid and allow the continent to be taken seriously in the world of economics and politics. He has also helped to broker peace deals in regional conflicts among Rwanda, Burundi, and the Democratic Republic of Congo.

But although Mbeki has assumed the role of one of Africa's most important leaders, his primary focus, of course, is his own country. Given his background in economics, it seems logical that helping to mend South Africa's economy will be one of his top priorities.

When the ANC took power in 1994, they inherited an economy in shambles. A combination of a high-spending apartheid government, as well as the difficulties caused by worldwide economic sanctions against the apartheid government, left an economy in dire need of assistance.

Nelson Mandela and the "prisoner" generation of ANC leaders had emphasized a Socialistic cure to the nation's problems. This meant that they felt that it was the role of government to help the poor directly, by redistributing the wealth from the rich to the poor, and by allowing large amounts of government spending to provide for the poor. Thabo Mbeki, and his generation that had studied economics in Western universities, shied away from this brand of Socialism. In its place, they embraced Western-style market economics.

As the Cenral Intelligence Agency (CIA) Factbook summarizes it, "South African economic policy is fiscally conservative, but pragmatic, focusing on targeting inflation and liberalizing trade as a means to increase job growth and household income." In other words, under Mbeki, the government would do what it could to help business grow, thus encouraging job growth that would, in turn, hopefully help to bring prosperity throughout the nation.

This policy has forced the ANC to walk a fine line. While the policy pleases the white-dominated business community, some members of the ANC feel that the government does not do enough to assist the impoverished black majority. Thabo, though, explains his policies in Africanist terms, believing strongly in empowering black South Africans rather than encouraging dependency on the government.

And, to a large degree, his policies have been a success. While employment and black poverty remain high, the economy

In Johannesburg, a child in Alexandra—known as "Dark City"—bathes in a plastic bucket on the doorstep of her home. Although Mbeki has funded urban regeneration projects for the area, Dark City residents live in squalor.

overall has grown. Because of this, most South Africans remain loyal to the ANC and to Mbeki's government. The majority seem willing to see economic transformation and redistribution of wealth as a long-term, ongoing process.

But while Mbeki's economic policies have been largely successful, other aspects of his presidency have been mired in

MBEKI'S VIEWS ON THE CAUSES AND TREATMENT OF AIDS HAVE BEEN SUBJECT TO WORLDWIDE CRITICISM.

controversy. Primary among these has been his government's handling of the AIDS crisis.

MBEKI AND AIDS

Among South Africa's other ongoing problems, including poverty, rampant crime (caused in no small part by severe poverty), and the scars left by apartheid, AIDS looms large. The figures regarding AIDS in South Africa are startling. According to the CIA, as of 2003, 21.5 percent of the adult population is infected with HIV/AIDS. Five million three hundred thousand people are living with AIDS. Three hundred seventy thousand people have died because of HIV/AIDS. Fifty percent of people in South Africa's hospitals have HIV. Obviously, it is a major humanitarian crisis for the nation and for the entire world.

Mbeki's views on the causes and treatment of AIDS have been subject to worldwide criticism. In April 2000, he publicly defended a small group of dissident scientists who claimed that HIV is not the cause of the disease. Mbeki has described AIDS as a "disease of poverty," and has argued that political attention should be directed to poverty in general, rather than at AIDS specifically.

Some have speculated that due to colonial dominion and control of Africa, as well as his life in exile, Mbeki feels that the very idea of AIDS is racially slanted against Africans. He once said, as quoted by Helen Schneider and Didier Fassin, "Convinced that we are but natural-born, promiscuous carriers of germs, unique in the world, they proclaim that our continent is doomed to an inevitable mortal end because of our unconquerable devotion to the sin of lust."

Unfortunately, this view struck a chord with many throughout Africa. Many Africans find it suspicious that such a large number of black Africans suffer from AIDS, and feel that the drugs that treat it, manufactured by Western pharmaceutical companies, are too expensive. In addition, South Africa has had a history of health policies that have ignored the needs of black South Africans. To some extent, such suspicions are not completely surprising.

In addition to voicing such suspicions about AIDS, Mbeki also briefly supported the use of a South African experimental drug called Virodene, which was later proved to be ineffective. And, his Health Ministry is headed by Dr. Manto Tshabalala-Msimang, who has promoted the treatment of AIDS through nutrition; he has also emphasized the potential dangers of the antiretroviral (ARV) drugs that have been used as treatment with great success throughout the world.

Fortunately, under the current South African system, the cabinet can override the president. It declared as cabinet policy that HIV *is* the cause of AIDS. And then, in August 2003, it promised to formulate a national treatment plan that would include antiretrovirals. Critics, though, have complained that the Mbeki administration has been slow to get the drugs to people in need and has failed to respond adequately to the epidemic.

Indeed, in August 2004, Tshabalala-Msimang confirmed that the government would not be able to reach its meager goal of supplying ARVs to just 53,000 people by March 2005. In her statement, quoted in *Thabo Mbeki and the Battle for the Soul of the ANC*, Tshabalala-Msimang made clear her distrust of ARVs. "If you say to the nation that you are providing ARVs then you will wipe out all the gains made in the promotion of a healthy lifestyle and prevention."

AIDS activists demand support from the South African government in a demonstration on June 8, 2005. Thabo Mbeki has been criticized for his treatment of the AIDS crisis in South Africa.

In addition, in the December 22, 2006, issue of *The Week* magazine, it is reported that Ms. Tshabalala-Msimang has said that she has more faith in lemon, beetroot, and garlic than in any drugs. In fact, South Africa's booth at an AIDS

On April 27, 2004, Thabo Mbeki is sworn in to a second term as president of South Africa. Mbeki is only the second black president of the country.

conference in Toronto in 2006 featured displays of garlic, beetroot, and potatoes.

Along with his health minister, Thabo Mbeki still remains unconvinced, despite his own government's official position, that HIV causes AIDS. Unfortunately, many other prominent ANC officials share this view. As Smuts Ngonyama, the party's official spokesman and a close associate of Mbeki, said in an interview with the *Star*, "It's based on a scientific assumption, and like all assumptions, it can be disproved."

THE FUTURE

Despite the controversy regarding AIDS, continuing high levels of unemployment, crime, and poverty, Mbeki was reelected to a second term as president in 2004. The majority of the South African people still trusted the ANC, which had led the fight to end apartheid, to continue its efforts to improve life for all South Africans.

As the South African Constitution now stands, Mbeki is limited to two terms of office. And although some have accused him of hoping for a change to the Constitution that would allow him to serve a third term, he has always denied this. In February 2006, Mbeki told the SABC that he and the ANC have no intention of changing the Constitution. He also stated, "By the end of the year 2009, I will have been in a senior position in government for fifteen years. I think that's too long."

Thabo Mbeki has devoted his entire life to the cause of South African liberty. He was separated from his family, spent years in exile, and endured the disappearance and likely murders of his brother and his only son. Despite this, Thabo persevered, determined to do everything within his power to help bring about an end to the evil of apartheid. And, thanks in no small part to his efforts, apartheid did come to an end. The South African people are now free, and their future is now in their own hands.

On the occasion of the adoption of the Republic of South Africa Constitution Bill 1996, Mbeki made what is perhaps his most famous speech, known as "I am an African." In it, Mbeki reveals his pride in being African, and his profound optimism in a bright future for South Africa and all the African people. It says in part,

Thabo Mbeki has devoted his entire life to fighting for a free South Africa. As he said in his moving 1996 "I am an African" speech, "Whatever the setbacks of the moment, nothing can stop us now!"

Today it feels good to be an African. It feels good that I stand here as a South African and as a foot soldier of a titanic African army, the African National Congress, to say to all the parties represented here, to the millions who made an input into the processes we are concluding, to our outstanding compatriots who have presided over the birth of our founding document, to the negotiators who pitted their wits one against the other, to the unseen stars who shone unseen as the management and administration of the Constitutional Assembly, to the advisers, experts and publicists, to the mass communication media, to our friends across the globe—congratulations and well done!

I am an African.

I am born of the peoples of the continent of Africa.

The pain of the violent conflict that the peoples of Liberia, Somalia, the Sudan, Burundi and Algeria bear, is a pain I also bear.

The dismal shame of poverty, suffering and human degradation of my continent is a blight that we share.

The blight on our happiness that derives from this and from our drift to the periphery of human affairs leads us in a persistent shadow of despair.

This is a savage road to which nobody should be condemned.

This thing that we have done today, in this small corner of a great continent that has contributed so decisively to the evolution of humanity says that Africa reaffirms that she is continuing her rise from the ashes.

Whatever the setbacks of the moment, nothing can stop us now! Whatever the difficulties, Africa shall be at peace! However improbable it may sound to the skeptics, Africa will prosper!

Whoever we may be, whatever our immediate interest, however much we carry baggage from our past, however much we have been caught by the fashion of cynicism and loss of faith in the capacity of the people, let us err today and say—nothing can stop us now!

CHRONOLOGY

1488 Bartolomeu Dias sails around Cape of Good Hope, becoming first European to do so since ancient times.

1652 First Dutch fort built in Table Bay at Cape Town.

1795 British seize control of the Cape Town, gaining final control in 1814.

1835 The Great Trek. Several groups of Boers move off into the interior of the country in search of great independence.

1869 Discovery of diamonds at Kimberley.

1880 First Anglo-Boer War, known to Afrikaners as the "War of Independence." The war ends with the Boer victory at Battle of Majuba Hill, February 27, 1881.

1899 Second Anglo-Boer War. The war ends with the signing of the Treaty of Vereeniging on May 31,1902, with the Boers acknowledging British sovereignty.

1910 The Union of South Africa unites the former Boer republics with the British-dominated Cape Province and Natal.

1942 Thabo Mbeki born on June 18, son of Govan and Epainette Mbeki.

1948 National Party takes power, beginning era of apartheid, separating whites and blacks.

1953 After fire and storm nearly destroys the family business, Mbeki moves to Queenstown to continue

his education. There he lives with his uncle,
Michael Moerane.

1956   Begins high school at Lovedale College.
Joins ANC Youth League.

1959   Expelled from Lovedale as a result of student strikes,
protesting Bantu Education Act. Moves home to
continue his education.

1960–1961   Completes British A-level examinations.
Involved in underground activities for the ANC.

1961   Elected secretary of the African
Students Organization.

1962   Leaves South Africa with other students on
instructions from the ANC. Went to then
Southern Rhodesia (now Zimbabwe), then
Tanganyika (now Tanzania), and finally to England
to study. While in England, continues his work
in mobilizing students in support of the ANC.

1964   Defendants in the Rivonia Trials, including
Govan Mbeki and Nelson Mandela, are sentenced
to prison for life.

1966   Receives his master's of economics degree,
University of Sussex.

1967–1970   Works for the ANC office in London. Undergoes
military training in the Soviet Union.

1971   Assistant secretary to the Revolutionary Council
of the ANC in Lusaka.

1973   Sent to Botswana, where he is among the first
ANC leaders to have contact with members of the

Black Consciousness Movement. His efforts help to bring them into the ANC.

1974 Marries Zanele Dlamini.

1974 Leaves Botswana for Swaziland as acting representative for the ANC. Active in mobilization and creation of underground structures.

1975 Elected to National Executive Committee (NEC) for the ANC.

1976 Sent to Nigeria as representative of the ANC. Plays major role in assisting students from South Africa to relocate in an unfamiliar environment.

1978 Leaves Nigeria and returns to Lusaka. Becomes political secretary in the office of the ANC.

1984–1989 Director of the Department of Information and Publicity.

1985 Serves as director of information and as secretary for presidential affairs.

1985 Member of delegation that met with the South African business community.

1989 Leads the delegation that held "secret talks" with the South African government in Switzerland.

1990 South African president F.W. de Klerk, on February 2, gives his famous "unbanning" speech, freeing political prisoners and legalizing the ANC and other liberation movements.

1993 Elected as chairperson of the ANC.

1994   Named by Nelson Mandela as executive deputy
        president of the South African Government of
        National Unity (May 1994–June 1999).

1997   Elected president of the African National Congress,
        December 18.

1999   Inaugurated as president of South Africa, June 16.

2004   Reelected to second term as president of South Africa.

BIBLIOGRAPHY

"ANC Youth League Manifesto—1944." www.anc.org.za/youth

Barrow, Greg, "South African Split over AIDS." http://news. bbc.co.uk/1/hi/world/africa/126941.stm

"Biography of Thabo Mbeki." ANC Web site. www.polity.org/ za.html/people/mbeki.html?rebookmark=1

Gumede, William Mervin. *Thabo Mbeki and the Battle for the Soul of the ANC.* Cape Town: Zebra Press, 2005.

Hadland, Adrian, and Jovial Ranto. *The Life and Times of Thabo Mbeki.* Cape Town: Zebra Press,1999.

Hadland, Adrian, and Jovial Ranto. *They Fought for Freedom: Thabo Mbeki.* Cape Town: Maskew Miller Longman Ltd., 2000.

Jackson, Derrick, "Ronald Reagan: A Serial Liar With a Heart of Darkness Who Made Americans Feel Good About Themselves." www.afro.com

"Mzabalazo: A History of the African National Congress." ANC Web site. www.anc.org.za/ancdocs/about/ umzabalazo.html

"Nelson Mandela." *Time Magazine—The Time 100—Leaders and Revolutionaries,* www.time.com/time/time100/ leadership/profile/mandela3.html

"The Scourge of AIDS in Africa." *The Week,* pg. 13, December 22, 2006.

FURTHER READING

Blauer, Ettagle, and Jason Laure. *South Africa (Enchantment of the World, Second Edition)*. Conn.: Children's Press, 2006.

Connolly, Sean. *Apartheid in South Africa*. Austin, Tex.: Raintree Steck-Vaughn Publishers, 2003.

Cottrell, Robert C. *South Africa: A State of Apartheid*. New York: Chelsea House Publishers, 2005.

Crompton, Samuel Willard. *Nelson Mandela*. New York: Chelsea House Publishers, 2006.

Domingo, Vernon. *South Africa*. New York: Chelsea House Publishers, 2003.

Mandela, Nelson. *Long Walk to Freedom: The Autobiography of Nelson Mandela*. Boston: Back Bay Books, 1995.

Pogrund, Benjamin. *World Peacemakers—Nelson Mandela*. San Diego, Calif.: Blackbirch Press, 2003.

WEB SITES

African National Congress
www.anc.org.za/

The Apartheid Museum
www.apartheidmuseum.org

DATA
www.data.org

PHOTO CREDITS

INDEX

ABOUT THE AUTHORS

DENNIS ABRAMS is the author of numerous books for Chelsea House, including biographies of Barbara Park, Anthony Horowitz, Hamid Karzai, Eminem, Beastie Boys, and Ty Cobb. He attended Antioch College, where he majored in English and Communications. He currently resides in Houston with his partner of 18 years.

ARTHUR M. SCHLESINGER, JR. is remembered as the leading American historian of our time. He won the Pulitzer Prize for his books *The Age of Jackson* (1945) and *A Thousand Days* (1965), which also won the National Book Award. Professor Schlesinger was the Albert Schweitzer Professor of the Humanities at the City University of New York and was involved in several other Chelsea House projects, including the series *Revolutionary War Leaders*, *Colonial Leaders*, and *Your Government*.